TOO CLOSE
FOR COMFORT

PAUL M. INSEL is Senior Research Scientist at the American Institutes for Research and Clinical Assistant Professor of Psychiatry at Stanford University. HENRY CLAY LINDGREN is Professor of Psychology at San Francisco State University. Both are authors of books and research articles on social psychology.

TOO CLOSE FOR COMFORT
The Psychology of Crowding

Paul M. Insel / Henry Clay Lindgren

A SPECTRUM BOOK

PRENTICE-HALL, INC., Englewood Cliffs, New Jersey 07632

Library of Congress Cataloging in Publication Data

Insel, Paul M
  Too close for comfort.

  (A Spectrum Book)
  Bibliography: p.
  Includes index.
  1. Crowding stress. 2. Personal space.
  3. Environmental psychology. 4. City and town
  life. I. Lindgren, Henry Clay, joint
  author. II. Title.
  HM291.I59   301.18´2   77-15670
  ISBN 0-13-925164-2
  ISBN 0-13-925156-1 pbk.

A Spectrum Book

10 9 8 7 6 5 4 3 2 1

Printed in the United States of America

Prentice-Hall International, Inc., *London*
Prentice-Hall of Australia Pty. Limited, *Sydney*
Prentice-Hall of Canada, Ltd., *Toronto*
Prentice-Hall of India Private Limited, *New Delhi*
Prentice-Hall of Japan, Inc., *Tokyo*
Prentice-Hall of Southeast Asia Pte. Ltd., *Singapore*
Whitehall Books Limited, Wellington, *New Zealand*

TO SIS WITH LOVE

Contents

Preface

Do people behave differently when they are crowded? Does living under crowded conditions affect attitudes, personality, and the ability to think and solve problems? Is crowdedness a threat to mental and physical health? If the answer to these questions is "Yes," are we humans sufficiently adaptive so that living in a crowded society will eventually make little difference in our lives? After carefully reviewing the evidence, we have concluded that crowding has serious consequences and is a contributing factor to the deteriorating quality of life.

Our interest in crowding and related problems grows out of our work in personality and social psychology, cross-cultural psychology, and especially social ecology. Social ecology is a relatively new discipline concerned with the interaction between the physical and social aspects of the environment. It is linked to traditional concerns of social psychology regarding the significance of the social environment and its effect on attitudes and values, intellectual development, and personal growth. Social ecology goes a step further in its concern with identifying and developing optimum human milieus. It attempts to find answers for such questions as "Is there an ideal level of population best suited to human functioning?"

The state of the art at present does not permit a clear answer to this question, but it does enable us to identify the major elements on which answers will eventually be based. In this book we have examined these elements and related issues in the light of research findings that have accumulated over the last decade. In doing this, we have made a deliberate attempt to present our interpretations and conclusions in language that we believe is clear, unobtrusive, and nontechnical, without less of scientific integrity. Crowding, be it in the form of world overpopulation or urban congestion, is one of the most pressing problems facing us today, and it cannot be solved unless both scientists and nonscientists understand it and work together on the issues and questions it poses.

We would like to express our appreciation to our wives, Marcia and Fredi, for their contributions as co-researchers and critics of the manuscript in its developmental phases. We would also like to thank the American Institutes for Research and the Psychology Department of San Francisco State University for providing social and intellectual environments in which we have found both the stimulation and the facilities that have made meaningful work possible.

Introduction

Chapter 1

The word "crowding" conjures up visions of being hemmed in, thwarted, elbowed out of the way—perhaps even trampled in a surging crowd. The thought of crowdedness leads to fantasies of escaping to a safe and secluded sanctuary—perhaps a desert island. The possibility of having to cope with crowds stimulates schemes and strategies that will enable us to avoid the press of superfluous and oppressive others. In short, the word *"crowding"* is loaded with negative connotations and carries more than a hint of personal danger. "Far from the madding crowd's ignoble strife" was not the most lyrical line that Gray wrote, but it certainly is the most famous, for it reflects a widespread if not universal feeling about crowds and crowding.

Crowding is an inescapable feature of life in an overpopulated world. It is the inevitable result of runaway birthrates, of the burgeoning of great cities and metropolitan areas, and of rapid and efficient modes of transit that enable large masses of people to aggregate in football stadiums, in factories, at rock concerts, and inescapably, in traffic jams.

Crowds are always composed of faceless others. A *group* can be "we," even a large one, but a *crowd* is always "they." The crowd that is "they" may be quiet and orderly, but pent up within its formless body it holds the possibility of unbridled destructiveness. When a crowd becomes a mob, there is little that an individual caught up in it can do to stem its headlong rush into fury or panic. To be a member of an outraged or frightened crowd is to lose one's identity. Self-control and common sense melt away before the intensity of the collective feeling.

Crowding, crowdedness, and crowd are therefore potential sources of anxiety in a world that has much to be anxious about. Hence it is difficult to view them without some twinges of antipathy, some predisposition to see them as potential threats to our security, well-being, and perhaps even survival.

POPULATION EXPANSION

Take one aspect of crowding, the population explosion. Many people, especially in the Western world, are concerned these days that the population of the world appears to be increasing at a rate that will exhaust the resources available for life support within decades. One estimate, made in 1960 and based on world population growth during the past two thousand years, predicted that Doomsday—the theoretical saturation point—will arrive in 2026, and more recent data suggest that we are ahead of schedule. It is easy to find scapegoats for this state of affairs, but difficult to get anyone to do anything about it. Industrialized nations, whose populations are nearly stabilized or growing very slowly, are critical of underdeveloped nations, whose populations are growing rapidly. Underdeveloped nations are resentful of this imposed responsibility to curtail growth and say, in effect, "If you would share your resources and help us, we would be as prosperous as you and our birth rate would taper off as yours has done." It seems ironic that when the standard of living rises, the rate of population growth decreases. Wouldn't people feel freer to have more children if they could better afford them? Not necessarily. When people see the possibility of a less shackled life, with more opportunity to explore themselves and their environment, they are less likely to allocate time and energy to raising children. However we appear to be at an impasse, and the international conference held in Bucharest in 1974 on population control was more concerned with political ideology than problem solving and hence provided little reason for hope that anyone will do anything constructive in the foreseeable future.

The problem of continued population expansion seems at first glance to be entirely an economic one, but closer examination shows that it goes far beyond economics. If the problem were solely a matter of achieving a balance between supply and demand, underdeveloped nations would quickly see that their resources cannot support the millions they now have, let alone the millions and millions more as yet unborn. To avoid famine and disaster, they must drastically reduce demand through birth control and increase supplies by whatever means possible. This is the solution being urged by industrialized countries, who have achieved a more or less happy balance between resources and demands.

The people of underdeveloped countries, however, view population growth quite differently. At the personal level, having families is related to such concepts as self-affirmation, competence, fate, and self-esteem, as well as the desire to receive support and reassurance from being surrounded by one's own kind, especially one's children. Perhaps the need for excitement and stimulation, coupled with a longing for some escape, however fleeting and temporary, from the tedium and unremitting drudgery imposed by poverty is also involved. The leaders of these nations, even though they might covertly hope for ways of bringing population and resources into balance, are helpless. Most of them rest on a narrow power base and are highly unstable; hence, they are unwilling to challenge popular opinion on this score. Furthermore, the means of dealing with the motivational aspects of population control are simply not available. The heads of government have no choice but to accept uncritically what the people tell them: "God has given us a bountiful number of children; as it is beyond our limited means to support them, the responsibility is yours." As the economic resources of the governments in most instances are extremely shaky, they naturally pass on the responsibility to wealthier countries which, they claim, have been able to maintain their affluence only at the expense of poorer countries.

The people of industrialized countries of course deny that they have any responsibility other than that dictated by normal humanitarian motives. Furthermore, they cannot see how anyone, poor or otherwise, would welcome the crowding that results from unbridled population growth. And so, they make token gifts and loans and counsel forebearance and self-restraint.

Actually, we ought to be able to understand why the people of any country, industrialized or otherwise, would take pleasure in population increases. It was only yesterday that the American people were delighted by census reports showing that we had finally reached the two-hundred-million mark! In those halcyon days, city fathers pointed with pride to the fact that the population of their town had doubled since the last census, while residents of Boston or San Francisco felt somewhat let down to read that the flight to the suburbs had caused a drop in their city's population. Even today a great many Americans are pleased to see the population of their city or state increase and are depressed by decreases. But when the increase takes place halfway around the world in some unenlightened tropical country, the shoe is on the other foot, of course.

PSYCHOLOGICAL FACTORS

The problems of crowding are therefore not merely economic but psychological as well. They are psychological because they concern the well-springs of human behavior: people's attitudes, feelings, values, needs, and percepts. If we are to gain any useful perspective on these problems, it will be through understanding their motivational factors. This is not to say that the economic and political aspects of the problems are irrelevant, but rather to say that they cannot be solved solely in those terms, without dealing with their psychological aspects. The point is especially important because the psychological aspects of social problems are usually overlooked or brushed aside as having only a minor, nuisance value. The wreckage of programs and schemes scattered along the course of history is mute evidence of the almost universal tendency to attempt the solution of human problems without anticipating the possible effects that motivation will have on human behavior.

Our ability to cope with population growth rests in part on our ability to understand the psychological dimensions of crowding and population density, for they are significant elements in the apparently suicidal behavior of the people of poor nations. Our misunderstanding of overpopulation is, however, only one example of how faulty concepts of crowding may cause us to misinterpret the behavior of ourselves and others. One problem is a confusion of the concepts of crowding and density, an issue we will take up in Chapter 2. Another problem is our tendency to use culturally toned percepts of crowding and crowdedness as a kind of smokescreen to obscure aspects of problems that we do not want to perceive, for one reason or another.

Some of these smokescreens are more obvious than others, of course. When a young man at a cocktail party turns to a young woman he met only five minutes earlier and says, "Let's get out of this crowd," we know that he is not so much objecting to the crowded situation as he is expressing a desire to take her where there would be fewer distractions and less public exposure. And when Mr. Dennis says that he would like nothing better than to leave his position as art director of a large, bustling advertising agency and head for a remote mountain lake, "where there isn't another human being in ten miles; where there is no telephone, no mail service, no TV, and the radio reception is lousy; and where I don't have to listen to idiot clients, idiot bosses, and idiot staff," we know there is more afoot than a simple desire to escape crowding.

Mr. Dennis' picture of a secluded retreat has wide appeal these days. Almost everyone we meet responds positively to the possibility, hope, or dream of a week or two or maybe a month during which one can "get away from it all," escape the crowds and throngs of everyday life, and "commune with nature." In such an Eden, "every prospect pleases and only man is vile," to cite the words of a nineteenth-century hymn. The only sounds are the wind in the trees, the lapping of little waves, and the occasional sounds of wildlife. Mr. Dennis' fantasy may be only an escape mechanism, but it is one that most of us can identify with.

Crowding is not merely a condition that we have all dreamed of escaping; it seems to be the cause or result of a great many of the world's ills. We do not have to go to underdeveloped countries to find negative effects of crowding; they are figuratively or literally just around the corner in the congested inner city or in the trailer camps and shantytowns of migrant workers.

Crowding seems everywhere to be identified with some kind of pathology. In impoverished areas it is associated with a high incidence of crime, physical and mental disease, unemployment, school learning failures, and child neglect. In more affluent surroundings crowding seems to lead to frustration, irritation, boredom, restlessness, as well as to a high incidence of suicide, divorce, drug abuse, alcoholism, obesity, and the whole gamut of "white-collar" crime.

The catalog of disasters and misfortunes attributed to crowding in its several forms is both long and varied. War is at the head of the list. The invasions that brought an end to the Roman Empire are ascribed to German tribes' being crowded off the plains of what is now southern Russia by pressure from the Huns. Overpopulation is cited as a prime cause of the series of military adventures into the Middle East known as the Crusades. Overpopulation and congestion are given as reasons for the military aggressiveness of the Aztecs, as well as their predilection for human sacrifice. And one of the reasons that we eye the underdeveloped nations apprehensively is our fear that crowded conditions resulting from unbridled population growth will push them over the brink into a war of global dimensions.

History tell us of one classical instance of crowding that touched off a war that had a long-range effect on the fortunes of two major countries; England and India. During the first part of the eighteenth century, the British operated trading posts in Bengal under privileges granted them by the Moghul emperor in Delhi. The Moghul government was militarily and politically weak, however, and the de facto control of Bengal province was taken over by its *nawab* or governor. By the middle of the century, the nawab became increasingly concerned by the growing power of the British and accused them of going beyond the privileges granted them earlier by the Delhi government. The British of course maintained that they were doing nothing to exceed the agreed-upon limits. Uneasy about the nawab's antipathy and growing power, however, the British then took the additional and wholly illegal step of fortifying their trading posts. This move was considered the final straw by the nawab, Siraj-ud-Daulah, who ordered his military forces to capture the trading post at Calcutta with all its personnel.

The account of what happened next is somewhat confused. It is said that some European soldiers became drunk and attacked the local people and that the nawab asked how this sort of thing would have been handled if the British had been in charge. He was told that they would have been thrown into the Black Hole, an eighteen-by-fifteen-foot punishment cell in the fort. The nawab apparently concluded that it would be a good idea to consign *all* the British he had captured to the Black Hole as a warning, or perhaps he intended to use it as a repository until he decided what he wanted to do with them. In any event, either the nawab or his lieutenants ordered the captives herded into the Black Hole. It was a hot and steamy night, and the only ventilation was that provided by a single window. Some say that 146 people were confined in the cell; more recent investigation suggests that there were 64, including at least one woman. Whatever the actual number, only twenty-one (one report says twenty-three) were alive the following morning. When news of the atrocity reached Robert Clive in Madras, he lost no time in mounting a counterattack that defeated the nawab, recaptured Calcutta, and firmly nailed down Bengal Province as the keystone of what was to become the British Empire of India.

It is probable that the nawab or his officers had little idea that an overnight stay in a densely crowded cell would have such fatal consequences. If living conditions in eighteenth-century Bengal were anything like those of today it is quite likely that what was impossibly overcrowded for a European was considered normal by Bengalese. Indeed, there is some evidence that the death toll in the Black Hole was the result of the prisoners' trampling one another in a panicky attempt to get near the window, rather than suffocation, as was widely believed in England.

In time, the account of the Black Hole of Calcutta in its most exaggerated form became a classic in English horror stories. Not only was it the dastardly act of rascally natives who dared to challenge British power, but the vision of the crowded cell aroused a special degree of revulsion in a country that was engaged in a pervasive and long-range love affair with wide-open spaces—through nature walks, field sports, cross-country running, and windows flung open on days that weakling outlanders felt were downright freezing.[1] The Black Hole atrocity also appeared particularly repulsive to the middle-class Britisher, whose preference for privacy and dislike of close interpersonal contact are justly celebrated. It was the ultimate example of what is likely to happen under crowded conditions.

It is worth noting that the English word *"crowding"* has no real equivalent in other European languages. The word derives from the Anglo-Saxon *crudan*—to thrust or shove. It still has much of its original meaning, in some instances, but along the way it has picked up an association with *throngs,* where pushing and shoving are likely to occur.[2] European languages have words for crowds of people or things, as well as words for pushing or shoving, but they lack a portmanteau word that includes the concepts of losing freedom of movement, being hemmed in, having one's privacy invaded,

---

[1]Countless bedroom windows all over the world have been flung open by well-meaning Britishers, with the admonition, "Now, we don't want this to become a Black Hole of Calcutta, do we?" This penchant for freezing bedrooms does not seem to exist on the Continent, where windows are kept tightly shut as protection against the unspecified dangers of the night air. The Black Hole atrocity is, after all, part of the British, not the Continental, heritage.

[2]From the Anglo-Saxon *thringan,* to crowd, and related to the German *dringen,* to press forward.

and running the risk of being elbowed aside. The fact that only an English word, *crowding,* implies all these things, suggests that the British are more likely to worry about such matters than are people in other cultures. Americans have of course taken *crowding* over from the British, together with its load of special meanings.

EFFECTS OF CROWDING

Although other Europeans may think that the British are inclined to overreact to physical closeness by feeling crowded in social situations that others would feel were normally populated, they nevertheless take crowding as a phenomenon that merits serious concern as a contributing cause of undesirable events. Some assign crowding more importance than do others, of course. Hitler was able to convince a good many people that crowding was a major threat to German destiny. He rationalized his expansionistic dreams by claiming that Germans needed more *Lebensraum*—living space—dismissing as unimportant and irrelevant the fact that the "living space" he had his eyes on was already occupied. The point here is that his propaganda was believed, which suggests that a good many in his audiences felt that they were crowded. This is an example of how a stated desire to escape from a crowded situation can serve as a smokescreen to conceal other motives.

Population experts note that wars may reduce crowdedness by decimating populations, but wars also create crowding by displacing people and creating refugees who often are required to live in exceedingly congested quarters until some means can be found to assimilate them. Sometimes the sojourn in refugee camps is relatively brief, as it was in most of the Western European countries after World War II, but sometimes it can last for generations, as it has in the Palestinian refugee camps.

Crowded living conditions are also blamed for crime. The most dangerous areas of a city are those which are the most congested. These are also the areas that are likely to have the highest incidence of diseases, both mental and physical. Within the crowded inner city, malnutrition and child abuse are common; wages are lower and unemployment rates are higher. The children who grow up in these densely populated areas have more than their share of difficulties in school. They are more inclined to have reading problems, to have poor attendance records, and to be identified by teachers as "problem cases." We shall have more to say in later chapters about relationship between urban congestion and social pathology.

CLASS SIZE AS A CASE STUDY

Although most teachers have a problem case or so to deal with, the most pervasive complaint they have about their work environment is that their classes are crowded. It is *class size,* rather than problem children, that inevitably comes up for discussion when teachers negotiate with school boards. As a result of such pressures, American school boards over the years have reduced the mean class size from forty-five pupils after World War I to about twenty in the mid-1970s. These figures are averages, of course, which obscure the fact that class sizes even today may run into the forties in some subject areas or schools and down to less than ten in others. In spite of this progress, teachers still feel that their classes are crowded, and class size remains an important item on the lists of demands presented by teachers' unions and is often a major cause for calling a strike.

At first glance, it might appear that teachers want to reduce class size because they think they are overworked and want to cut down on the number of papers they have to correct or the records they have to keep, but such an interpretation overlooks the psychological stress that ordinarily results from dealing with several dozen youngsters simultaneously. Even when classes are on their best behavior, teachers are under a considerable degree of internal pressure to carry on the programs of instruction for which they are responsible and at the same time to cope with the needs, expectations, demands, and problems of each individual child. The greater the number of pupils in a class, the greater the number of potential distractions, both for the teacher and for each learner as well. Trying to carry on a program of work and at the same time decide which distractions to respond to and which to ignore can be extremely wearing. Everyone has to deal with crowding as a part of daily life, but few have to work under such crowded conditions. Hence, it is quite understandable that teachers should want to exercise control over this aspect of their work environment.

But it is not always clear exactly what teachers mean when they complain about crowded classrooms. Paul Gump (1975), a psychological ecologist at the University of Kansas, recounts an anecdote that suggests that teachers may not be thinking of crowding in its conventional sense. The anecdote also illustrates some of the complications that arise when planners try to create new work settings. Gump's story describes the fate of a new school constructed with "open classrooms."

For a number of years some of the more avant-garde specialists in elementary education have been extolling the virtues of open classrooms. What they have been saying makes a great deal of sense on logical grounds, namely, that children who would ordinarily constitute the first, second, third, and fourth grades in a school can be assigned to a room much larger than the conventional size, a room that can be richly supplied with learning centers, audiovisual equipment, and special resource materials—far more than would be possible in a single classroom. As a consequence, some elementary school buildings have been constructed with classrooms four times the usual size in order to accommodate ungraded classes. It is also argued that such classrooms create *large open spaces* that permit greater flexibility of educational planning and programming, as well as fluidity of movement, on the part of individuals and groups.

In telling this anecdote, Gump draws a diagram of such a classroom as it was initially conceived, providing space for over a hundred children, four teachers, and a wealth of educational resources. Then he shows the room two years later. Behold: it is no longer a classroom with large open spaces, for each of the teachers has "taken back" the children in her grade, withdrawn with them into one corner of the room behind barricades of wooden screens, chalkboards, and bookshelves.

The reasons for this development are obvious, once one thinks it over. It was difficult to get any work done in the larger area. Life was just too noisy, too turbulent. Children were more than usually restless and distractible, and they experienced problems in attending to assigned or even self-imposed tasks. Now, behind the barricades, they find considerably less self-selection of activities and less individual freedom, but more work can be done with less psychological cost. Perhaps there *was* more learning in the open arrangement, but teachers were not sure of what kind or how much. They were less aware of what was going on and less able to evaluate the results of their work. In effect, they felt that the open situation kept them from "doing their jobs," so to speak. It is important to note not only that the rearrangement is more crowded and congested, but also that it is the kind of crowding that teachers can manage.

As far as the average or "normal" classroom situation is concerned, there is a continuing debate between educators and taxpayers and among educators themselves as to how many children a teacher should be expected to teach. Teachers have complained about psychological stress and overwork, but their most telling argument has been the claim that children could learn better in smaller classes. Research into the relationship between class size and learning scores is, however, rather equivocal. Some studies report that pupils make greater gains in larger classes, making it appear that crowding may have no deleterious effects and that a certain amount of it may even provide an advantage. This is all very confusing for harassed, overworked teachers, as well as for laymen who want the best for children. What is clear is that the relationship between crowding and school learning is a much misunderstood phenomenon.

Studying this dilemma of the educator and the enlightened layman indicates how difficult social-psychological problems can be that directly or indirectly involve crowded environments. Because teachers experience difficulties in dealing with large groups of children, they might make class size the villain for all kinds of school problems. If children are not learning as much as they are expected to, class size is a convenient scapegoat.

THE STUDY OF CROWDING

In this respect, teachers are not much different from the rest of us. As crowding makes us uncomfortable and a great many social ills occur in crowded environments, it is easy for us to hold crowding responsible. Our ability to deal with social pathology may be hampered by our conviction that crowding is a bad thing. People in other cultures seem to put up with a great deal more crowding than we do and may even think it desirable. Further, at rock concerts, sports events, carnivals, and the like we actually seek and enjoy the experience of being crowded.

It is our plan to present crowding as not only a social and ecological phenomenon but as a subject with many psychological contrasts. In the forthcoming chapters we will explore some of the interesting contrasts between urban and rural life. How do people living in a city like New York cope with the constant stimuli that bombard them? How do they interact with the hundreds, even thousands of people encountered daily? Does the high population density found in cities deform or lessen the quality of life? Or do crowds and swarms of people inject a stimulating, exciting quality to urban living? We will discuss the social climate of the congested urban area compared to the less populated town. Just like people, cities and towns have personalities of their own. Some people are stimulating and vivacious; some cities are exciting and alive. Some people are composed and have well-ordered minds; some cities or towns are orderly with clear and explicit regulations.

We will review the animal studies that relate to crowding and consider the extent to which these studies are relevant to human experience. We know that lower animals have territorial instincts that shape very explicit kinds of behaviors. To what extent does "territoriality" influence human behavior?

We will examine the experimental studies relating to crowding and high-density situations. Many investigators have attempted to discover the effects of crowding on such things as judgment, cooperation and competition, mental development, and psychological adjustments.

Why do people vary in their feelings about being crowded? Some people will deliberately select a crowded area over an equally convenient less-crowded area.

The issue of privacy is intimately related to the concept of crowding. It is a need, unrecognized by many, that most of us have. Whether achieved through solitude, intimacy, or anonymity, it can serve to unwind us from tense states or to provide a release from too many interactions and distractions.

The problem of crowding varies not only from person to person but also from culture to culture. The Arabs, for example, differ significantly from the British in the way they treat spatial distances.

Clearly, crowding has many dimensions and facets that require close examination if we are to cope adequately with problems that involve population density, architecture, urban living, and the congestion of everyday life.

Crowding:
Difficult to Avoid;
Hard to Define

Chapter 2

In the year 1799, Daniel Boone left his home in the raw frontier state of Kentucky and moved to uncharted land west of the Mississippi River, saying, "Too crowded! I want more elbow room!"

The kind of living space that Daniel Boone thought was too crowded would be viewed as being sparsely populated by most Americans today, and probably by those of Boone's day as well. But his views illustrate one of the problems we encounter as we try to understand crowding and the effect it has on human behavior, namely, that it is difficult to define crowding in a way that satisfies everyone. The tavern which appears noisy and congested to George seems pleasantly busy and active to Mike. The closeness of others that seems stifling to Sue as she rides to work on the bus she finds pleasant and exciting when she rides around the lake on a holiday weekend with a dozen friends crowded into a small motor launch. The crowdedness that George objects to in the tavern and Sue dislikes in the bus are not the same, and both also differ from the crowdedness that Boone complained about. Furthermore, Boone's complaints were based on experience covering months and years, while the reactions of George and Sue are focused on smaller units of densely populated space, experienced over much shorter periods of time.

Problems of definition always arise when behavioral scientists study problems of human experience. The language we tend to use in describing these problems is fairly loose, consisting of simple and direct terms that have a great deal of meaning in everyday life but that prove to be complex when scientific investigators attempt to plan experiments and construct reliable measures. What we refer to as crowding is in this respect no different from aggression, love, learning, and hunger—all concepts which carry a heavy freight of attitudes and feelings, which are defined scientifically in a variety of ways and are still being redefined by researchers and theoreticians.

We shall therefore take the coward's way out by not attempting to construct a definition of crowding that would in the end satisfy no one. We shall instead talk about crowding as though everyone understands 'what it means. We have ample precedent for this approach. Some fifty years ago, psychologists attempted to define "intelligence," were unable to come up with a description that satisfied anyone, and agreed not to define it. "Intelligence," they concluded, "is what we measure when we administer intelligence tests." This nondefinition resolved the problem, and everyone cheerfully went about his research without further argument about the exact nature of the variable they were studying.

The tests designed by the psychologists did indicate that concepts of intelligence all had a great deal in common. They all involved thinking and problem solving in one form or another. Similarly, the research of psychologists dealing with crowding indicates a common factor, the number of individuals in a given area, the measure referred to as *social density.*

SOCIAL DENSITY

For the purposes of research, social density has a great advantage, for it can be measured precisely in terms of the number of individuals per square yard or meter of space in a given location or in terms of the amount of space separating individuals who are standing, sitting, working, talking, or whatever. Equating crowding with density also has logical appeal. Common sense tells us that the more individuals there are in a given area, and the closer they are together, the more likely they are to feel crowded. Presumably, the more crowded they are, the less effective, productive, or happy they will be and the more anxious, irritable, and unfriendly they will act.

When a high degree of social density, or crowding, is both chronic and widespread, we refer to it as overpopulation. Zlutnik and Altman (1972) note the following common beliefs about the deleterious effects of overpopulation:

1. *Physical effects:* starvation, pollution, slums, disease, physical malfunctioning, and breakdowns.
2. *Social effects:* poor education, inadequate physical and mental health facilities, crime, rioting, and wars.
3. *Interpersonal and psychological effects:* drug addiction, alcoholism, family disorganization, withdrawal, aggression, and diminished quality of life.

Zlutnik and Altman's review, written in the early 1970s, commented that virtually no research data existed to support these beliefs. Psychologists have in recent years attempted to remedy this deficiency. Although most of their research has focused on social density as experienced by subjects over relatively brief periods of time, some studies have had a somewhat broader scope. Eoyang (1974), for instance, was interested in both density and reduced privacy and the effects they had on the attitudes and feelings of students living in a trailer park on the Stanford University campus. The trailers were identical: each had three bedrooms, two bathrooms, a kitchen, a living room, and a dining area. In some trailers, each occupant had a bedroom to himself; other trailers were more congested, and bedrooms were shared. Ghetto residents might consider such quarters palatial and spacious, but replies to the interviews Eoyang conducted made it clear that most of the students felt cramped.

As might be expected, the greatest dissatisfaction with living arrangements tended to be expressed by individuals living in trailers that had the most occupants, while those in sparsely populated trailers were likely to express the highest degrees of satisfaction. Students who enjoyed the privacy of unshared bedrooms also tended to rate their housing more favorably than those who shared their bedrooms with others.

But the replies were far from uniform. Some students living in crowded trailers and sleeping in shared bedrooms rated their accommodations as better than those whose living arrangements provided more space and more privacy. Such differences were not unexpected, however. People who occupy the same trailer are like other small groups of individuals, which vary somewhat with respect to the compatibility of their members as well as in terms of their members' expectations, personality traits, and previous experiences.

The only personal factor that seemed to have any relevance in this study was the size of the student's family. Those students who had grown up in small families were inclined to express unfavorable opinions about their living arrangements, whereas those from large families were more favorably disposed. Although Eoyang's findings are interesting and generally consistent with what we would expect from common sense, they are, after all, summarized reports of subjective feelings. Hard-nosed, skeptical scientists are inclined to ask: "Does social density make a significant difference in the way people behave—in their productivity, for example?"

The research unfortunately provides us with no clear-cut answer to this question. A study conducted by Emiley (1975) is typical. He assigned male students to experimental conditions of high or low social density and had them work for forty minutes on the assembly of an erector set. When Emiley asked them afterward about their reactions, students who had worked in the high-density setting rated their working space as less satisfactory and more crowded than did those assigned to the low-density setting. There was no difference, however, between the two groups of subjects in their success in performing the assigned task, nor was there any difference in their reported enjoyment of the experience.

This outcome is surprising. People who are aware that they do not have sufficient work space and who say that they feel crowded are not expected to perform as adequately as those who work in more spacious surroundings. In any event, they are not supposed to enjoy the experience. We can, of course, explain away these findings by saying that the fun the students had in working together at the task of putting the erector set together more than compensated for the discomfort of their work setting. It is also quite possible that their uncomfortable environment led them to try harder and thus turn out an adequate performance. These are speculations, of course, and we cannot be sure.

The results of such experiments suggest that research studies limited specifically to density that do not take into account motivational factors may be wheel-spinning activities that are not going to tell us much about the general effects of crowding.

PSYCHOLOGICAL FACTORS

Zlutnick and Altman (1972), like other critics of crowding research, have been justifiably scornful of the social density approach. Studies exclusively concerned with social density simply do not tell us enough, or if they tell us anything it is that density has to be related to other aspects of the human condition. In real-life social situations, density is never experienced as an isolated variable. It is always in association with other aspects of everyday experience: mood, attitudes toward those who share the space, the task at hand, and so forth.

The fact that crowding involves elements over and beyond density has been examined by Stokols (1972), who pointed out that density is a purely physical measure of the number of people per unit of space, whereas crowding is a psychological concept, involving past and recent experiences, feelings, and motives.

Density, according to Stokols, is a necessary but not sufficient condition for the feeling of being crowded. He also distinguished between *nonsocial crowding,* being cooped up alone in a small space, and *social crowding,* a condition resulting from the presence of too many people, as well as between *molecular crowding* (crowding in a relatively small area, such as a home) and *molar crowding* (large-area crowding, as in an urban setting). This distinction between molecular and molar crowding is especially important, because, as we shall find, the results of studies indicate that the effects of the two kinds of crowding are quite different.

Although Stokols' distinction between density and crowding is useful, it leaves psychologists somewhat in a quandary when it comes to conducting research. As we noted earlier, it is relatively easy to deal with density as a variable, for investigators can expose subjects to various degrees of openness or restriction in space or can populate a given area with as many individuals as the space will hold, but dealing experimentally with the many elements that can turn density into crowding is not easy.

Some attempts have been made, however. Fisher (1974) conducted a study which took into account subjects' attitudes toward those with whom they share social space. Previous research by Byrne (1971) had found that an individual is attracted to others to the extent that he perceives them as sharing similar attitudes and values. In Fisher's experiment, undergraduates were informed that certain individuals (actually confederates of the experimenter) had attitudes that were similar or dissimilar to theirs. These confederates then interacted with the subjects at one of four distances. Results showed that, in contrast to those conversing with "dissimilar" confederates, students who interacted with "similar" confederates judged their environment to be more aesthetically pleasant, reported feelings that were generally more positive, and, most importantly for our present discussion, perceived themselves to be less crowded. The important finding of Fisher's research is that when we are physically close to the kind of people we like, we are inclined to feel less crowded than when we find ourselves in the midst of people who do not attract us.

Although clever researchers can, like Fisher, measure the effect that liking or being attracted to others has on our behavior, it is only one factor out of many that may influence the degree to which we feel crowded. Even when we are with people we like, we may reach a point when, because physical contact with them is very close and/or has been prolonged, we feel overly saturated with conversation or whatever fun-and-games we have been engaging in. The prospect of an evening of cheek-by-jowl closeness with otherwise attractive others can appear dismal or boring if we are in the mood to enjoy a few uncluttered hours of reading and quiet music. Thus, while studies of interpersonal attraction can tell us something about the likelihood of feeling crowded, there is much that they leave unexplained.

PERSONAL SPACE

A dimension of crowding that seems less subjective than interpersonal attraction but not so cut-and-dried as density is what Zlutnik and Altman (1972) term "interpersonal crowding," referring especially to events and situations in which individuals are unable to exercise adequate control over their interactions with others and/or in which the psychological or physiological costs of controlling these interactions are too high. Invasions of personal space and territory are good examples of this aspect of crowding.

Personal space was brought to the attention of behavioral scientists by Hall (1959, 1966), who noted that cultures differed from one another in the amount of interpersonal distance they considered appropriate. He observed, for example, that Americans tend to prefer greater personal space than do members of Middle Eastern or Latin American cultures. We shall have more to say about this in Chapter 3.

Sommer (1959, 1969) was the first to conduct experiments in which the personal space of unwitting subjects was "invaded." It was thus possible to measure the limits of that "invisible envelope" or "bubble of space" in which each of us lives, whose boundaries mark the optimal distance at which various kinds of interpersonal exchanges should occur. When our personal space has been invaded, we are likely to react with discomfort, anxiety, irritation, and even anger and aggression.

In Sommer's research, female experimenters approached female students seated alone at library tables. If the experimenter sat down several chairs away, she was ignored; but if she sat down next to the subject, the victim displayed signs of discomfort. She would draw in her arm or head; turn away from the intruder, exposing her shoulder and back; or mark off her territory with books, purse, or coat (Felipe and Sommer, 1966). The obvious interpretation of this reaction is that the victim felt uncomfortable and was seeking to shield herself from further invasion.

Baxter and Rozelle (1975) conducted a study that demonstrates dramatically what happens when our personal space is invaded. The experiment was conducted with male undergraduates who volunteered to role-play a citizen being interviewed by a policeman. The role of the policeman was played by a graduate student who had been trained to conduct an eight-minute semistandardized interview of a type that a policeman might conceivably carry out. The interview began with a few general questions dealing with the subject's identity, whereupon the subject was asked to give a full and complete description of the contents of his wallet. He was then asked to produce the wallet in order to check his memory of its contents. The "policeman's" manner was subdued and polite throughout.

The researchers divided the interview into four two-minute phases. The "policeman" initially stood four feet from the subject. Then he closed the distance to two feet for two minutes, moved even closer to within eight inches for two more minutes, and finally moved back to a distance of two feet. The "policeman's" move to within eight inches of the subject ordinarily would have been considered unusual, but it was timed to coincide with a request that the subject produce his wallet and hence could be interpreted as a visual check on his accuracy in describing its contents. However, the interviewer did not look at the wallet but rather maintained eye contact with the subject during this stage, as he did throughout the eight-minute session.

The behavior of subjects during this type of interview was compared with that of subjects who went through the same procedure except that the "policeman" came no closer than two feet.

The behavior of the subjects in both types of interviews was videotaped so that their reactions could be coded and analyzed by the investigators. The analysis showed that the amount of movement on the part of subjects in the second or comparison interview declined over the eight-minute period. They were obviously accommodating to the unusual situation and were feeling less tense.

The students in the first set of interviews, however, showed signs of increasing restlessness, especially when the "policeman" closed the distance to eight inches. They clearly interpreted this move as an invasion of personal space, for their speech became noticeably disrupted and was characterized by an uneven flow and a jerky, staccato pattern. They also displayed other indications of discomfort and tension: They glanced away frequently, fidgeted, and moved around a great deal.

Baxter and Rozelle interpreted their results very conservatively, even cautiously. The behavior of the subjects in the first type of interview, they said, may not have reflected discomfort, for it may have been defense or escape maneuvers. Only the deterioration of the speech patterns, they said, could be considered as a certain indicator of uneasiness, and they pointed out that other signs of anxiety, such as tics (involuntary, meaningless motions) or noticeable stiffness or awkwardness in movements were absent.

We should note, however, that each interview lasted only eight minutes, with the severe crowding phase lasting for only two minutes. The fact that the subjects displayed an increased degree of activity consistent with protection and escape even during this brief period suggests that they were beginning to feel uncomfortable. Otherwise, why try to escape?

In the course of our everyday activities we seldom approach others face-to-face as closely as within eight inches, thus violating their personal space, but instead we avoid such obvious discourtesies. We engage in the appropriate maneuvers automatically, without any awareness of our attempts to refrain from infringing on

personal space. Here is an example, drawn from a field study conducted by social psychologists, of how we avoid such violations in
everyday life.

Let us imagine ourselves walking down a hallway ten feet wide,
bound on some errand or other. We pass a shallow alcove in which
there is a bench. If someone is sitting on the bench, we will detour
slightly away from him as we walk by, even though no part of his
body protrudes into the corridor. If two people are seated on the
bench, we will make a greater detour, and the presence of three
bench sitters will lead us to give them as even wider berth. Our
tendency to vary the size of our detour in accordance with the
number of bench sitters makes it appear as though personal space
has additive properties, as if the invisible space bubble surrounding three bench sitters bulges farther out into the hallway than
that occupied by only one or two persons.

Knowles and his fellow researchers (1976), who monitored the
behavior we have just described, also found that when they showed
subjects maps of the corridor, alcove, bench, and sitters and asked
them to pencil in the paths they would take down the hall, the
paths they traced were similar to those the investigators had observed
in the actual situation: The more people sitting on the bench, the
more the path deviated from a straight line.

Such studies make it clear that personal space has well-defined
and generally agreed-upon characteristics. When its boundaries
are violated, we usually become uncomfortable and take defensive
measures. And, conversely, we avoid invading the personal space
of others. The greater the number of others, the farther we will go
out of our way to avoid them.

The reason that we change direction while walking and avoid
coming close to people who are standing or sitting is that we do not
want our personal space to overlap with theirs. If this were to
occur, both we, the walkers, and they, the standers or sitters, would
feel some degree of discomfort or tension.

To the lay person, it might seem difficult to secure scientific evidence that such violations of personal space do indeed produce a
measurable degree of tension, but we should never underestimate

the ingenuity of the social psychologist who wants to get to the bottom of things. In this connection, Middlemist and his co-workers (1976) deserve some kind of accolade for a study that demonstrated not only that invasions of personal space produce tension but also that the degree of tension could be measured with some exactitude.

Middlemist and his fellow investigators set up their observation stations in a men's lavatory. There were three urinals in the washroom, which made it possible for them to observe the behavior of unsuspecting subjects under three conditions of crowdedness: alone, in the company of a urinal user two spaces away, and in the company of a user at the adjacent urinal. The investigators manipulated the degree to which subjects' personal space was invaded by employing a confederate to stand at the appropriate urinal and at the same time blocking whichever urinal they wanted inactive by placing washing equipment in its basin and hanging an "out of order" sign on it.

An observer concealed in a toilet stall, using a periscope that permitted him to observe the subject's lower torso, employed a stop watch to time the unzipping of each subject's fly, the initiation of the stream of urine, and the cessation of the process.

In contrast to the performance of the control subjects who were lone users of the washroom, subjects who shared it with a confederate standing two urinals away required more time to start the urine stream and also urinated more briefly. The greater degree of inhibition, however, occurred in those subjects who were standing at a urinal next to that used by the confederate.

It is clear, of course, that more than personal space is involved in the Middlemist study. The inhibition that results when individuals are "coactively engaging in private elimination," to use the researchers' phrase, occurs because of a feeling that one's privacy is threatened or, to some extent, invaded. The fact that this type of privacy invasion is a routine occurrence does not mean that it has no effect, as the Middlemist study shows. We tolerate it, but we cannot help but feel some degree of awkwardness.

Altman (1975) would agree with this assumption. After reviewing the available research dealing with people's reactions to crowding and invasions of personal space, he concluded that privacy was what mattered most to them. Privacy is not merely the absence of others, according to Altman, for he defines it as the "selective control of access to oneself or to one's group" (p. 18). He goes on to describe it as a kind of process whereby we manipulate our interpersonal boundaries, a maneuver that individuals or groups employ in order to manage and regulate their relations with others.

Both personal space and territoriality, which we shall discuss shortly, are, in Altman's view, mechanisms we use to achieve the levels of privacy we desire. We may extend or pull back the invisible boundaries that set off our personal space or territory; we can use them to keep others at what we consider a safe or comfortable distance; or we can encourage others to approach and even touch us. We can set off our boundaries clearly so there can be no mis-understanding— "so far and no farther," or we can weaken there and make them permeable as an invitation to confidentiality and intimacy. In short, by signaling the state of our boundaries, we indicate our degree of openness to others, thus communicating the degree of our receptivity to personal interaction.

Privacy has traditionally been thought of in a defensive sense, that is, in terms of exclusion of others, seclusion, withdrawal, and avoidance of interaction. But Altman feels that these aspects of privacy have been overemphasized and that the positive aspects have not been adequately studied. It is through employing the mechanisms of privacy, he says, that we are able to observe and deal with ourselves without the distraction of others' input. It is privacy that permits us to carry out self-evaluation, a fundamental process in attaining self-understanding and self-identity.

Altman considers self-identity to be central to human existence. "For a person to function effectively in interaction with others requires some understanding of what the self is, where it ends and begins, and when self-interest and self-expression can be exhibited" (p. 50). Privacy mechanisms enable us to define the limits and boundaries of the self, and when our privacy goals are not achieved, or must be achieved at an extravagant cost, psychological or other-wise, we feel crowded.

TERRITORIALITY

There are important differences between the two mechanisms of personal space and territoriality that we employ to attain privacy goals. Whereas personal space is the invisible bubble that accompanies us wherever we go and that may expand or shrink, as the occasion requires, territorial behavior involves a place or an object identified as belonging to a person or group. Often we mark the place or object in a way that puts others on notice as to our territorial rights. The fact that we can lay claim to territory—a home, an office, a desk, a bed, a chair, or whatever—makes it possible for us to withdraw at times from the distractions of having to cope with others' input and engage in the self-evaluation and contemplation that are basic to self-understanding and identity.

Territoriality has other uses, of course. It reduces ambiguity, confusion, and indecision by providing us with previously determined areas in which we can carry on our daily work and perform other more-or-less routine activities. Life in a complex, fast-moving society would be impossible unless its members could function within the framework of formal and informal sets of agreements as to who belongs where and who is the rightful owner or user of a given object. As Altman says, "Personalization and ownership are designed to regulate social interaction and to help satisfy various social and physical motives" (p. 107).

Territoriality has attracted a great deal of attention in recent years, largely because of the writings of ethologists, such as Lorenz (1966) and Tinbergen (1968), who sought to explain human behavior in terms of data derived from their observation of animals. Aggression in both humans and animals, ethologists have declared, is the result of attempts to defend one's territory against actual or threatened violations. This view, which has been popularized by Ardrey (1966, 1970), has been criticized by Altman, who pointed out that there are many differences between human and animal territoriality. The essential difference is that human territoriality is much more complex. Any human being lays claim to many more territories than does any animal and uses them in ways that have nothing to do with biological survival—for recreational purposes, to give one example. Many territories are occupied only temporarily, such as tables in a restaurant or classrooms at school. Furthermore, it is very common for human beings to withdraw when such territorial claims are challenged by others. Irritation even anger is a frequent response, to be sure, but actual physical aggression is relatively rare. Edney (1974) has also pointed out that humans routinely permit the presence of others on home territories without antagonism. The rituals of entertaining and visiting are common examples of this.

Still another difference between humans and animals is that human territoriality is four-dimensional, in the sense that it involves time as well as space. We apologize before intruding on another's time. "Can you spare me a minute?" we ask. And the harried parent of a brood of active youngsters sighs, "If I only had a few minutes for myself!"

In spite of their differences, however, human territoriality and animal territoriality have this in common: They provide for security. That is, they permit members of groups to enjoy the advantages of living in close proximity and at the same time to avoid confusion and anarchy. It is when systems of territoriality do not work very well or break down under the stress of circumstance—extreme and prolonged social density, for instance—that social situations develop pathological overtones.

It is a popular position these days to condemn territoriality and property rights as divisive or even inhuman. Such a view is unrealistic, for when territorial boundaries are poorly defined or group members become overly permissive about the violation of boundaries previously maintained, everyday existence takes on a quality of instability and unpredictibility and the experience we call crowding becomes inevitable. Just as crowding leads to anarchy, anarchy eventually leads to crowding. As Robert Frost once wrote: "Good fences make good neighbors."

Privacy, therefore, is based on the territorial integrity of time-and-space boundaries and is the opposite of crowding. When two or more individuals share the same living quarters, some agreement about the "ownership" or priority of access to certain locations and objects is necessary. Without territorial agreements, the co-residents are always sorting through each others' clothing and other personal belongings, uncertain where to place themselves or their possessions, using up resources the other had counted on, and the like. Without the traffic management permitted by territoriality, there inevitably are collisions and confusions, with resultant irritation and resentment.

Some interesting data regarding the relationship between territoriality and privacy have emerged from a study conducted by Rosenblatt and Budd (1975), who asked married and unmarried cohabiting couples to complete an interview schedule which included the following questions:

> Do you have your own separate bed (a bed that both of you recognize as yours to sleep in) or side of the bed?
> Do you have a certain and separate area of the closet in which you store your own things?
> Do you have certain and separate drawers of a dresser or chest in which you store your things?
> Do you have a certain and separate portion of the bathroom to place items such as your toothbrush?
> Do you have a certain and separate chair to sit in at the dinner table?

Analysis of the replies of the subjects indicated that married couples were significantly more "territorial" than unmarried couples, even taking into account such factors as the amount of time the couples had lived together. It seemed clear from the results that the two kinds of couples had somewhat different expectations regarding their arrangement. It was as though married couples had concluded, tacitly or otherwise, that if their relationship was to endure, they could not take the risk of leaving territorial issues unresolved. Unmarried couples, on the other hand, evidently had consciously or unconsciously determined that the relationship was to be temporary and hence saw little point in raising territorial issues. Another interpretation is, of course, that they sensed that staking territorial claims and setting boundaries would be tantamount to committing themselves to a long-term relationship that neither wanted.

In addition to the questions about territoriality, Rosenblatt and Budd asked each subject if he or she had a special place within the residence for being alone. Married and unmarried couples also differed in the reply to this question, for unmarried subjects were more likely to reply in the affirmative and married subjects in the negative.

The researchers interpreted this difference to indicate that unmarried individuals had a greater need of a backstage area, coupled with needs for symbols of separateness and relative freedom from togetherness pressures. It was as though they had left some problems of interpersonal relations unresolved by their avoidance of territoriality, problems that in the end had to be dealt with by each individual's withdrawing and shutting the door, actually and figuratively, in order to exclude the partner. Although this practice prevailed in the homes of unmarried couples, it was rare in those of the married ones. Even those couples who had lived together before marriage reported no more need for places of private refuge than did the couples who had not cohabited before their marriage.

Arrangements for privacy are no substitute for territoriality, if an intimate relationship is to continue. Rosenblatt and Budd observed that the tendency of their unmarried couples to avoid territoriality was likely to be a continuing source of problems and that it could become a significant source of estrangement, leading to termination of the partnership.

EXPECTATIONS

The findings of Rosenblatt and Budd are consistent with the idea that crowding and other social density problems can be controlled or avoided by territorial arrangements or, in the absence of such arrangements, by resorting to self-isolation. An understanding of crowding and crowdedness, however, involves more than a grasp of how territoriality operates. Territorial arrangements can deal with the physical environment and with interpersonal events—the first two headings in Zlutnick and Altman's list of the dimensions of crowding—but are only indirectly related to the third element: the psychological or personal/subjective dimension.

We noted earlier that situations in which social density is high are sometimes regarded quite favorably by participants. When we are enjoying ourselves at a party or at the theater we are not likely to think of ourselves as crowded. On the other hand, our pleasure in the unspoiled beauty of a remote mountain lake is disturbed when we discover a tent a mile or so away across the expanse of water. If we have sought the isolation of the mountains in order to escape the hurly-burly of everyday life and "get away from it all," the appearance of another nature lover, however distant, is a jarring note that makes us feel crowded once again.

Clearly, whether or not we view a social situation as crowded depends on what we are prepared to accept. The expectations that we bring to any situation may be analyzed in a number of ways. Altman has suggested that the comparison level (CL) theory of Thibaut and Kelley (1959) is useful in this respect. In their discussion of the possible outcomes of a social relationship as experienced or anticipated by us, Thibaut and Kelley cite two important standards. One is the CL, the standard against which we evaluate the relationship, and the other is the comparison level for alternatives (CL_{alt}), the standard we use to determine whether to continue or terminate the relationship. In our discussion of the psychological element in crowding, we are principally concerned with CL, but admittedly CL_{alt} has some weight, for it determines whether we will view an uncomfortable situation as intolerable or decide to make the best of it.

Thibaut and Kelley use CL to indicate the standard by which we evaluate the rewards and costs of a given social relationship in the light of what we think we deserve. If the outcomes of the social situation exceed the CL, we are likely to consider it a satisfying one, but if it falls below the CL, it will appear dissatisfying and unattractive. One possibility, of course, is that we may consider the situation to be overcrowded.

What we "feel we deserve" from a given social relationship is based on such information as the type of social relationships we and our peers have experienced in the past, what we have expected of the relationship, what our options are, and whether we have sought the relationship or wanted to avoid it.

To use Daniel Boone once more as an example, his CL for evaluating the social situation he faced in Kentucky was based on his having roamed for years over vast ranges of forest land. Although his pioneering had opened the way for settlers, he probably had not anticipated that their presence would change his life style. He undoubtedly was unprepared for the rapid increase in Kentucky's population. The census of 1800, taken a year after Boone's departure for Missouri, showed 5.5 persons per square mile in the state of Kentucky. This was considerably less than the population density of 15.35 persons per square mile in the thirteen original states in that year, but it was a marked increase over 1790, when Kentucky contained fewer than two persons per square mile. By way of comparison, the 1970 census showed a density of 57.5 persons per square mile in the United States taken as a whole, and the figure for Kentucky was 80.

Boone's feeling of being crowded was no doubt aggravated by the knowledge that he could escape to more thinly populated territory west of the Mississippi. Without this CL_{alt}, he might not have viewed Kentucky as crowded.

Here is another example of how CL affects our judgment of whether or not we are crowded. Some of the poorest streets in Calcutta are lined with open-front, one-man stalls four or five feet wide and no more than eight feet from front to back, built into the lower story of buildings several stories high. The stalls, in which goods are sold, are "stacked" two deep, so that there are two layers of these shops, one layer at street level and the other immediately above it. The stalls in each layer are about four or five feet from floor to ceiling, so that a customer must bend down or squat to make purchases from a shop on the lower level or stretch up to deal with a shopkeeper at the second level. Sometimes the lower-level stalls are built a foot or two below street level to facilitate access. Some of the shops are retail establishments, selling cloth, hardware, or foodstuffs, and others are workshops in which tailors, metal-smiths, or woodworkers practice their trades.

People in most parts of the world would probably consider such working arrangements incredibly crowded, yet the observer looks in vain for the behavioral indicators of crowded discomfort—the defensive or evasive gestures noted by Sommer in his study of personal space in libraries or those recorded by Baxter and Rozelle in their simulated policeman-citizen interviews.

A number of elements in the situation experienced by these shopkeepers enable them to accept their situation with relative equanimity and to perceive it as uncrowded. For one thing, their stall is their territory, and its limits are clearly marked by walls, floor, and ceiling. Their identity within this territory is firmly fixed, and when they do not have customers, they have a degree of privacy. In determining the CL for evaluating their social situation at work, they are fully aware that their space is less congested than that of thousands of families who huddle together on nearby sidewalks. Considering also the fact that the living quarters of the Bengali poor are small and likely to contain sizable numbers of children and relatives, these tradesmen probably feel less crowded at work than they do at home. As long as they are in their stalls, they are insulated from invasions of personal space by family members. The social situation of these tradesmen is, furthermore, relatively stable, in the sense that it has not varied drastically over the past few decades. Nor are other and more attractive options open. Whatever other life styles are available to them are likely to be much less desirable than their present one. This does not mean that they are content, for they voice the universal complaints of living costs that are continually rising and income that never seems to catch up. There is too much crime, corruption in the government is an open scandal, and young people are not so industrious or respectful as they used to be. But crowding is not a major issue for them, because their CL tells them that they are about as well off in this respect as can be expected.

ADAPTATION

Studies of sensory adaptation also tell us something about the likelihood that people will feel crowded in a social situation. The sensory receptors in our bodies respond to changes in stimulation, but their output to the central nervous system diminishes as the new stimulation is maintained at the same level. A very hot tub bath is scarcely bearable for the first few seconds, but it quickly becomes comfortable.

The same phenomenon obtains with other kinds of stimuli. Human beings can adjust themselves to the sounds of rock music at ear-splitting intensity; to the thin air of twelve thousand feet elevation, and more; to the pitching decks of small fishing boats; to the hot, stale air of coal mines thousands of feet below the surface of the ground; and so on. The same may be said for social situations, in which our CL is based on what we have been used to and what we expect.

This tendency of human beings to adapt and to accommodate themselves to social situations initially experienced as uncomfortable is demonstrated by Sundstrom (1975), who conducted an experiment in which groups of six male students were crowded into a small room. The men interviewed each other in pairs. One member of each pair was a naive subject who did not know that his partner was a confederate of the experimenter. As the pair conversed, the confederate deliberately intruded on the personal space of the subject by leaning forward to a distance 14 to 18 inches from his partner's face, resting his hand or clipboard on his partner's knee, and making sustained eye contact. Each subject participated in six-minute interviews with three different confederates.

After the experiment, videotapes were analyzed in order to pick up behavioral clues as to the amount of discomfort subjects had been experiencing during the three interviews. In contrast to control subjects who had interacted with confederates who did not intrude, subjects whose personal space had been invaded were more likely to display behavior indicative of discomfort—but only in the initial interview. During the two remaining interviews, indications of discomfort declined to a point where they were actually less than that of the control group. In other words, the social experience that was initially somewhat repugnant to the subjects became more acceptable after a relatively brief period of exposure.

The results of Sundstrom's experiment are consistent with a series of studies conducted by Zajonc (1968), who has shown that with repeated exposure to a mildly disliked novel stimulus, subjects come to like it.

Adaptation and accommodation through continued exposure to initially noxious stimuli are of course only partial explanations of why social density is sometimes enjoyable and sometimes distasteful. Our CL is based not only on what we have become used to but also on what we expect or believe we are entitled to. It is this subjective —that is, psychological—element that seems to make the major difference between the congested social situation that is experienced as crowded and that which is ignored or even enjoyed.

In this connection, it can be argued that the students who participated in Sundstrom's experiment may have decided that the intrusiveness they were experiencing was all part of the research game and that they might as well "go along with the gag" and enjoy it. We can also conjecture that if the charade had continued for an hour or more, the novelty effect would have worn off and the subjects' reaction would have been boredom and even irritation. This psychological element seems to determine whether our personal space or territory has been invaded, or whether we have sufficient privacy in which to collect our thoughts and develop an adequate sense of self, as Altman would put it.

We have used the word "seems" in the foregoing analysis because of our lingering suspicion that this concept of crowding is both limited and misleading, even though it is the prevailing view of most social psychologists and is based on a sizable number of research studies. It is a view that might be expressed by such a formula as : Crowding equals a Density that is greater than our CL (C = D > CL). In everyday language this might read "social density is bad for you only if you think it is."

A major reason for questioning such a formulation is that people are not infallible judges of what is best for them. The history of drug abuse and addiction is only one example of how decisions based on subjective states can have self-destructive results. We have noted the universal human tendency to adapt to situations initially experienced as stressful. In other words, our ability to adapt to and even come to feel positive about crowded situations may lead us to believe that they are good for us, even when they are not.

An experiment conducted by Smith and Haythorn (1972) on behalf of the Navy and the National Aeronautics and Space Administration illustrates this point. Their research is especially significant because their subjects were observed not for a few minutes or hours, as in most social density experiments, but actually lived in cramped quarters and in isolation from the outside world for a period of three weeks.

Men participating in the experiment were assigned to two or three-man groups confined in specially constructed small rooms, some of which were made especially crowded by the installation of baffles and false walls. Data gathered daily during the three weeks indicated that men in the more-crowded quarters reported more symptoms of stress than did those who experienced less crowding. Three-man teams in the more-crowded quarters also reported a higher level of anxiety than did comparable teams in the less-crowded situation. The tendency of crowding to produce stress was also confirmed by the psychiatrist assigned to the project, whose interviews conducted after the 21-day period indicated that members of the three-man teams who lived in the more crowded quarters were the ones who showed indications of having experienced the greatest amount of stress.

These findings are hardly surprising. Common sense tells us that the greater the amount of crowding, the higher the degree of stress.

When we examine the personal reactions of the men, however, the results are surprising, for men in the more-crowded situations actually reported less hostility toward team members than did those in the less-crowded quarters.

What these sets of data suggest is that crowding does have negative effects of a psychological nature, but that those who are more crowded tend to accept the situation better. The more the stress, the better the adaptation, it seems. Perhaps we should revise our earlier statement to read, "Social density may be bad for you, even though you have come to accept it."

In everyday life, crowding seems to be a straightforward matter: You are either crowded or not, and you like it or you don't. The psychological studies we have reported indicated that crowding is not simple, that it is rather a very complex phenomenon. They show that it cannot be defined simply, in terms of social density, because people's attitudes are important. On the other hand, people's attitudes may not be an accurate index to the effects that crowding is having on them. There is no doubt, however, that attitudes and feelings about crowding are important, and in the next chapter we shall examine them further.

One Man's Party Is Another's Noisy Crowd

Chapter 3

As we indicated in our earlier discussion, how we feel has a great deal to do with whether we see ourselves as crowded. In psychological jargon, "how we feel" comes under the heading of *affect,* that aspect of behavior which includes feeling, emotion, attitude, judgmental standards, and values. Everyday experience is full of examples of the ways in which our affective state conditions the amount of distance or closeness we prefer with others.

If we are edgy and irritable at the end of a day, as a result of having tried to deal with too many people's demands, expectations, and problems, we may look upon the congestion around a cocktail bar as too crowded and hence escape to the solitude of a quiet evening at home. But if the work day has been humdrum and a bit lonely, or dull, a half hour at a lively bar becomes more inviting, and we do not think of it as crowded. In short, our tendency to view a social scene as crowded or not depends on our mood, which is in turn conditioned by immediate experience.

PERSONALITY TRAITS

A mood that results from a hectic or a dull day at work is directly caused by our environment and is only temporary, but some of our affective states are more persistent and may characterize almost everything we do. Betty is consistently energetic, always up to her ears in more projects than she can effectively handle. She is enthusiastic, seldom on time, and inclined to be preoccupied. Bob's characteristic mood is more subdued, to the point of being pessimistic, even somewhat depressed and gloomy. Jill is inclined to be competitive and just a bit edgy when she thinks she is being outmaneuvered, but Steve is cooperative to the point of going out of his way to give others the initiative and advantage.

These are but a few of the countless affective patterns that can be observed in individuals. Everyone displays such behavioral consistencies; we are of course more aware of them in others than in ourselves. These persistent and consistent affective patterns are what psychologists term *personality traits.* A great deal of the research of specialists in personality and social psychology is devoted to measuring and studying traits.

One personality trait that has been identified and measured is sensitivity to the close proximity of others, that is, to social density. Dooley (1974) first secured a measure of the reactions of male college students to the physical closeness of others by asking his subjects to walk one at a time toward a stationary target person until they began to feel uncomfortable about being too close. He then divided the subjects into two groups: those who stopped advancing sooner and who obviously preferred more space between themselves and others, and those who walked much closer to the target and who preferred less interpersonal distance.

Dooley then asked the two groups of men to participate in an experiment that required them to compete with others on a two-hour task requiring speed and accuracy in making judgments. Some of the subjects worked on the task in a high-social-density situation, in which there was very little distance between them and their fellows, while others were in a low-social-density situation, with considerable space separating the participants.

At the end of the two-hour session, the men were queried as to their reactions to the experiment. As might be expected, those who had been assigned to the high-social-density situation were much more likely to report feelings of being crowded, uncomfortable, and irritable. They were also inclined to complain about the unfriendliness and aggressiveness of the others in their group.

Although reactions of the subjects tended to differ according to the experimental condition they had experienced, differences were most pronounced when Dooley compared the reports of those who initially had been identified as preferring more interpersonal distance with those of the men who had preferred less. The men who had been the most hesitant when approaching the target person were the ones who found the high-social-density situation the most objectionable. They were more likely to report that the assigned task was less enjoyable and less interesting. An analysis of their performance, furthermore, showed that they were less successful than the other subjects.

When the experiment was over, all the subjects were asked to complete a proof-reading task, in order to monitor the after-effects of crowding. Once again, those men who preferred more interpersonal distance and who had been subjected to the socially dense situation were less accurate than the others; when all subjects were invited to participate in a follow-up discussion, they were more likely to decline.

What this experiment shows, then, is that people who do not enjoy physical closeness not only are more uncomfortable than others when they have to work in a socially congested situation, but also perform less well, an effect that persists for some time afterward. Crowded situations, therefore, have a more pronounced effect on some people than on others. The degree of crowdedness we sense or feel is to some extent relative to the kind of people we are.

This tendency to prefer more or less interpersonal distance is in turn related to other personality traits, which can be fairly easily identified and measured by psychological tests. Vanderveer (1973) administered personality tests measuring tendencies to be outgoing (extraversion) or inward-turning (introversion) to university students of both sexes. The subjects also took tests to determine their degree of social maturity and to detect traits characterized by overanxiety and tension—neuroticism, in other words.

The students were then told to imagine themselves as entering various kinds of social settings—a restaurant, for example. In some instances, the students were asked to think of the settings as about to fill up with people; in other instances, they were to expect that the settings would remain relatively uncrowded.

When Vanderveer analyzed the relationship between the personality test scores and the way the students thought they would react to potentially crowded or uncrowded situations, he found those who rated high on introversion and neuroticism scales were more inclined to say that they would engage in what might be called "defensive seating," by planning to select seats away from the center of the restaurant. They preferred seats in nooks and alcoves that would ensure the maximum in privacy and provide some protection against the anticipated influx of customers.

What Vanderveer's survey indicates, in short, is that the person who is shy and more than usually anxious about his relations with others is much more likely to be apprehensive about crowding and possible invasions of his personal space than is one who enjoys social interaction or is not especially upset by it.

Although Vanderveer's findings are consistent with what common sense already tells us about shy people and their behavior in social situations, we should not exaggerate their importance. We should not conclude, for example, that all defensive reactions to social density are pathological or that all attempts to seek out crowded situations are motivated by considerations of good mental health. In spite of the fact that Vanderveer's results met the usual standards for statistical significance, in actuality they accounted for only a small fraction of the possible range of human behavior. His research did show that people who are unusually threatened by having to deal with others are likely to feel especially hemmed in and crowded when surrounded by others, but it said little about the average person, who does not make extreme scores on the measures he used. The main point of his study is that the tendency to feel crowded is to some degree an individual matter in that some people characteristically find social density more stressful than others do.

The psychologist who wishes to study personality has many options open to him. He can focus on specific traits, like introversion or neurotic anxiety, or he can examine the kinds of traits that tend to be associated with people in various categories or classes. He can, for example, study personality differences between preadolescents and adolescents, or between adolescents and young adults. Or he can compare personality trait differences between culturally defined groups, like English-speaking and French-speaking Canadians. Research data on differing reactions to crowding on the part of the groups we have named are meager, and much research remains to be done, but a considerable amount of study has been devoted to the behavioral differences of two important groups: men and women.

Personality differences between the sexes have intrigued people-watchers from the very beginning of time. The general consensus is that some rather consistent differences exist between the sexes in mood and characteristic patterns of behavior, but there has been considerable disagreement as to what causes the differences. The conventional or traditional explanation is that feminine or masculine personality traits reflect physiological differences. Explanations on a simplistic level usually refer to differences in sexual organs and their functioning, while more sophisticated explanations take into account hormonal and neural differences between the sexes. The basic idea is the same in these two types of explanations, simplistic or sophisticated: It is that men and women, as well as boys and girls, display differences in both mood and behavior because they are born different.

This explanation has been challenged in recent years, and the view often expressed by members of the intellectual community of North America is that sex-related personality differences are *learned,* that is, they result primarily from differences in the ways that boys and girls are treated in their most formative years. These learned differences are further reinforced by a society whose expectations and demands on an individual are determined by his or her sex. If the differences are learned, this line of reasoning goes, they can also be unlearned.

It is beyond the scope of this book to examine and evaluate the data marshalled by proponents of the two schools of thought. As far as the student of personality is concerned, the research evidence is quite clear that, from toddlerhood onward, differences between any randomly selected, sizable groups of males and females are likely to be fairly well defined. We all know of individuals who do not fit the mold, of course, but we should keep in mind that these are exceptions to the general trend.

The results of psychological studies are monotonously consistent: The effect of sex on personality test scores is exceeded only by differences in age and perhaps by degrees of psychopathology. As a result, psychologists who construct and administer such tests conventionally report two sets of score norms: one for males and one for females. But for the present discussion, personality test scores are only slightly relevant, for what we are primarily interested in learning is whether sex has any relationship to attitudes and behavior with respect to crowded situations. The general finding is that it does.

Ross and his co-workers (1973), for example, conducted a series of experiments in which mixed-sex groups of university men and women conducted discussions in which they attempted to resolve dilemmas that the researchers had posed. The chairs of the students were set either 16 inches apart in a small room or five feet apart in a larger room. During the discussions, the students were observed through a one-way glass by the researchers, who took notes as to who looked at whom.

After the discussions, the students were asked to fill out questionnaires in which they reported their feelings about the stuffiness of the discussion room and the degree of physical comfort or discomfort they had experienced. They were also asked to report any indications of personal upset on the part of themselves or others in the group. Finally, they were asked to rate themselves and other members of the group on a number of personality traits, such as selfishness, calmness, goodness, and likability.

These responses were all examined for clues as to the students' attitudes and feelings about their experiences while participating in the experiment. Some fairly marked differences emerged from this analysis. The men who had carried on their discussions in the larger room were more comfortable, psychologically speaking, than those who had been in the smaller, more congested room, for they rated themselves and one another higher on such traits as likability, unselfishness, and calmness. Women reported the opposite views, for those who carried on their discussion in small, crowded rooms expressed more positive feelings toward themselves and others than did those in the less congested setting.

A check of the observers' notes also showed that women looked into the faces of other participants more frequently in the smaller room, whereas men looked at one another's faces more frequently in the larger one. The results make it clear that the women enjoyed the closeness and forced intimacy of the smaller room more, while the men were more at home in the openness and spaciousness of the larger room.

We might expect, in view of the theories about crowding examined in Chapter 2, that inasmuch as the women in this experiment responded more favorably to the smaller, more congested room, they would have been less likely to say that they found it crowded. An analysis of the participants' reports, however, indicates that there were no sex differences in this respect. In other words, women enjoyed the smaller room more *even though they saw it as crowded.*

The sex differences reported by Ross and his co-workers are not isolated findings. Epstein and Karlin (1975), for example, studied students at Rutgers University taking evening classes, a group whose average age was older than that of the subjects in the Ross experiment. The students were assigned to mixed-sex groups of six and asked to sit either in a closetlike room that measured only four feet by four feet or in a more spacious one that was 33 by 18 feet. The small room was so crowded that the students were in direct body contact with the people seated next to and across from them. In the spacious room, the distance between the chairs was 4½ feet and the rows of chairs were 7½ feet apart. Once the subjects had been seated, they were requested not to talk to one another, but to remain silent for a half-hour period. The purpose of this instruction was to increase the degree of psychological stress and tension.

After the half hour of mandatory silence, the students were brought to a normal-sized testing room, where they were allowed to select a seat and were given a number of tasks to work individually. One of the tasks required the students to assign points on whatever basis they wished to the individuals who had been with them during the first phase of the experiment, as well as members of another group of students now with them in the testing room. The purpose of this task was to measure the extent to which the students were attracted to one another.

The researchers were interested in seeing whether the degree of crowdedness the students had experienced would have any after-effect on the ratings that the students assigned to one another, as well as on the seating arrangements that developed spontaneously when the students were brought to the testing room. Their results showed that women who had been seated cheek-by-jowl with others in the smaller room were the ones who behaved in more socially cohesive ways (that is, group-supportive) when they were in the testing room. For one thing, they selected chairs in the center of the room in order to be close to other members of their recent group. Even though they had been huddled in a tiny room under conditions that were literally "too close for comfort," they seemed to feel an attachment to those who had gone through the experience with them. When it came to assigning points in the personal rating task, they were also inclined to give more points to members of their group rather than to the other students in the testing room.

On another task, which was constructed in such a way that subjects had either to cooperate or to compete with another partner, the women who had been in the crowded situation tended to be more cooperative than women who had not been crowded. Finally, the same women were more inclined than the other subjects to rate members of their recent group as "likable," "good," and "friendly."

The differences just described were most pronounced for women who had been seated in the middle of the rows of three subjects in the small room and who, as a consequence, had experienced the greatest amount of crowding.

The men in this experiment generally reacted in ways opposite to the women's. The effects were especially pronounced with those who had been in the crowded room, for they rated members of their recent group lower than did any of the other students and also displayed a higher degree of competitiveness; otherwise, the differences between this group of subjects and the others were less pronounced than in the case of the women who had been crowded. In other words, the crowding experience left the men merely somewhat edgier, but it had a pronounced effect on the women, who displayed a wide range of positive social behavior as a result.

Why does crowding affect men and women differently? Epstein and Karlin attempted to answer this question by proposing a hypothesis that men feel that they must adhere to a social norm that discourages displays of emotion and feeling, while women are permitted greater freedom in this respect. The need to suppress feelings thus causes men to dislike crowding, while the freedom to display feelings causes women to feel positive about it, according to this line of reasoning.

To test this hypothesis, the investigators asked the participants: "To what extent do you feel that your group encouraged a person to show signs of physical discomfort while in your group room?" The answers to this question indicated that the crowded men tended to believe that the group had discouraged display of feelings of discomfort, while the women in the same situation reported that the group had encouraged them to reveal how they felt. These replies, the researchers felt, suggested that the men and women were aware that if the norms for each sex were reversed, the sexes would react to crowding differently. In other words, if men did not suppress their feelings, they would enjoy crowdedness more, whereas if women suppressed their feelings more, crowdedness would not have so positive an effect on their behavior. Taking one more step beyond this observation, the investigators speculated that "were men to adopt norms of sharing distress and women to adopt norms of hiding distress, men would display more positive and women more negative behavior."

Whether because of the social norms we have learned or the hormonal balance and neural pathways that were wired into us at birth, such studies leave little doubt that men and women tend to respond somewhat differently to close interpersonal situations. The findings of these investigators are fairly consistent with those of researchers who have studied another area of personality; vocational interests. Data based on responses to the Strong Vocational Interest Blank collected for some 50 years show that women tend to find the helping professions—teaching, social work, and counseling—more attractive than men do. Men are more likely to be attracted to occupations in which the worker functions essentially on his own—engineering, forest service, research, and the like. Whether we say that social pressures or inborn differences in temperament or a combination of factors causes this depends on our personal convictions, that is, whether we lean toward a social or a genetic explanation in explaining sex differences.

Whatever the causes of such differences may be, the research data gathered by psychologists, sociologists, and anthropologists indicate that men and women in most societies form two somewhat separate subcultural groups marked by differences in speech, customs, social norms, personal and interpersonal style, and attitudes.

Two field studies demonstrate the kinds of findings that behavioral scientists report. In one investigation, a city supermarket was observed under three conditions of congestion: quiet, intermediate, and crowded. When the market was crowded, conventional patterns of shopping behavior tended to break down, and customers were more likely to act in inconsiderate ways toward one another and to display fewer signs of interpersonal concern. They were more inclined to outmaneuver and bump into one another, to edge into lines ahead of turn, and to apologize less frequently for having invaded others' personal space. Aside from this general trend, there was a clear difference between the sexes, for men shoppers were more inclined to adhere to conventional patterns of behavior than women were (Stark, 1973).

In an Australian study, pedestrians were observed as they walked in the "zebra crossing" (indicating the pedestrian right of way) across the square in front of the Sydney railroad station. The observers noted that men and women behaved as though they were people from two different populations, for their pattern of loco-motion differed markedly. Men tended to maintain a consistent rate of speed as they walked across the square, but women were more inclined to hesitate, speed up, and slow down. In contrast to the men, the women were likely to display forms of movement that were "perturbed," to use the term selected by the researchers (Henderson and Lyons, 1972).

Observers who have examined sex-related patterns of behavior in a variety of societies generally concur that sex-related patterns of personality and behavior are more marked in traditional cultures than in industrialized ones. Although these studies have given little attention specifically to crowding, they have produced some evidence to indicate that members of different cultures react differently to social density and invasions of personal space, which are of course basic elements in the social phenomenon we call "crowding."

SOCIAL NORMS

Some of the evidence is anecdotal, drawn from observations of the way in which people of different cultural groups seek or avoid close contact with others. As we play the role of the tourist, we are inclined to focus on superficial differences between cultures— clothing, language, architectural styles, food, and the like—and tend to overlook more subtle but nonetheless highly significant cross-cultural differences in the way people interact with one another. If, however, we live for long periods in another culture and come in close contact with its members, we are more likely to experience incidents that jar us into awareness of some of the more fundamental differences between our own culture and the life style of our host country. In such an event, we may discover differences in attitudes toward personal space and crowding, as did an Englishman who lived for some years in the Middle East.

Roger, our English friend, said that he really liked Arabs, really he did. He had lived in Arab countries for over twenty years, spoke Arabic, and spent much time with Arab friends. But he had a complaint. They did crowd one at times. Take the business of picnicking. He and his family would drive out into the Lebanese countryside on a Sunday, find a pleasant spot off the highway, and settle down for a nice picnic.

Within a half hour, whatever pleasantness and charm their picnic area had possessed when they found it had now vanished, for the family would be surrounded—even crowded—by Arab families who had been drawn to the spot as if by a magnet. They would drive by, stop with a squeal of the brakes, and unload their children and picnic baskets. It was all very friendly, you know, as though the English family had been just waiting for companionship so they could really enjoy themselves. The Arab families just couldn't bear to see the English family all alone in a wide grassy area, and they filled up the empty space as rapidly as they could.

"Now in England," said Roger, somewhat plaintively, "this kind of thing just isn't done. If you find an attractive picnic spot, passers-by respect your prior occupancy rights and move on in search of other locations. The Arabs are really very nice people, but they just don't understand that a chap needs some privacy."

Contrast this account with an anecdote from the other side of the coin—the experience of Yussuf, a young Saudi who came to the United States.

Yussuf was met at the airport by an American petroleum engineer who was a friend of his father's. The American drove him to a rather palatial ranch home in the hills just outside Los Angeles and showed him to his room.

Then he said, "I've got some things to do in town, and you've had a long plane ride, so why don't you relax and enjoy yourself? If you'd like to swim, there are suits in the dressing room just off the pool. If you'd rather read, here are the latest magazines. Or, if you'd like to go for a ride, just help yourself to one of the horses in the stables. I'll see you in a couple of hours, just before dinner." And he strode off.

Yussuf said he was deeply shocked and upset by this treatment. Back home, a guest was someone that the family made a great fuss over. They never left him for a minute, urging cigarettes and coffee on him, crowding around, hanging on his words, giving him the most solicitous care and attention. Leaving a guest alone was considered to be insulting, and he wondered what he had done or said to merit this rejection.

What Yussuf was experiencing, of course, was culture shock, the exposure to a new set of social norms. Giving a guest the run of the premises and leaving him alone to enjoy its pleasures is considered a friendly, hospitable gesture in America. Overwhelming a guest with attention and providing him with constant company is the norm in the Middle East.

This difference in social norms was noted by Hall (1959, 1966; see Ch. 2), a cultural anthropologist who was one of the first behavioral scientists to draw attention to the way in which people from different cultures vary in their attitudes toward personal space and its boundaries. His observations convinced him that English people, as well as Americans and Canadians, place a high value on privacy and apartness, but that Mediterranean people, including both Latin Americans and members of Middle East cultures, are not disturbed by the physical closeness of others and actually enjoy situations that North Americans and Northern Europeans consider to be hopelessly crowded and congested.

Hall's observations have received some support in research findings indicating that people from different cultures and subcultures vary in the boundaries they set for personal space. Little (1968) studied the interpersonal distances preferred by male and female Swedes, Scots, Greeks, Southern Italians, and Americans, by asking them to arrange pairs of dolls representing adults talking to each other. Little asked his subjects to recreate nineteen different conversational settings, such as "two people talking about the best place to shop," "two good friends talking about a pleasant topic," "a policeman questioning a person about some burglaries that have occurred in the neighborhood," and the like.

Little's findings pointed up some interesting intercultural differences. Scottish subjects, for instance, arranged the doll representing a policeman and the doll representing a woman in such a way that the distance between them represented the equivalent of slightly more than four feet, but Greeks set the proper distance between the same two individuals at the equivalent of two and one-third feet. Scottish women subjects were the most stand-offish, for they expressed preferences for interpersonal distances that were a third greater than the average for all the subjects. Physical closeness was valued most by Greek women, who were most comfortable when the space between conversationalists was about a third closer than the distance set by Scottish women.

These findings are consistent with Hall's observations, but Little's other findings were not. Little did find that subjects from Italy preferred less interpersonal distance than the average, but he also observed that Scottish men, Swedes, and American women set personal space boundaries at distances about an average for all the national groups, and American men expressed a preference for interpersonal distances that were closer than those of any of the populations sampled except the Greek women.

We can of course criticize Little's study on the grounds that the space people set between dolls may not be a close match for the way they will actually behave in real-life situations. We can also question whether his samples were really typical. However, those who wish their scientific findings to be neat and tidy will be relieved to learn of a field study conducted by Baxter (1970), who employed a team of observers to estimate distances between pairs of visitors to a zoo. An analysis of their data showed that people of Latin American background (as indicated by appearance and language) walked and stood about 1.8 feet apart, while the average distance for Anglo-Americans was 2.3 feet. Children visiting the zoo preferred more physical closeness than their elders did, for they walked or stood about 2 feet apart, while adults averaged about 2.5 feet.

Other research indicate that there are subcultural differences among children as well as among adults regarding personal space. One team of observers watched primary school pupils as they interacted on the playground and found that middle-class white children tended to stand about a foot apart, while Puerto Rican and black children from working-class homes preferred interpersonal distances of about six inches (Aiello and Jones, 1971). Evidently the excitement and activity of the playground is more conducive to close physical contact than is visiting the zoo.

In spite of the slightly jarring note sounded by Little's findings on American men, we are probably on safe ground to accept his view of basic differences in personal space preferences expressed by North Americans and British on the one hand and by Mediterranean and Latin peoples on the other. These variations may in turn be related to fundamental differences in ideas about individuality, personal rights, and privacy, an area of investigation that has barely been scratched by cross-cultural research. Nevertheless, intriguing scraps of evidence hint at some of the dynamics underlying this fundamental difference in views. We have, for example, the observations of Pollis (1965), a Greek sociologist, who pointed out that Western European (and American) concepts that envision the individual as having an existence to some degree apart from the rest of society, and even from his family and friends, are completely foreign to the Greek view of life. One indicator of this cross-cultural difference is that there is no word for "privacy" in Greek, which she maintains is fairly clear evidence that the concept does not exist in that culture.

People in other Mediterranean countries also seem to have little idea of the meaning of what we mean by privacy. In Spanish, "privacy" can be translated by "retiro" (retreat), "soledad" (solitude), and "asilamiento" (isolation)—all words that describe some of the physical characteristics of "privacy," but which completely miss the vital affective or feeling quality of the word. Italian uses much the same words to translate "privacy," but also includes "segreto" (secret). The sinister connotations of "segreto" are consistent with the suspicion with which Mediterranean people characteristically regard a person's attempts to secure or ensure privacy. To Mediterraneans, the only reason one might wish privacy is that one has something to hide. The idea that privacy might be desired for reasons of psychological comfort or for contemplation and self-assessment appears insubstantial and even ridiculous.

Privacy poses few problems in Northern European languages and cultures. In German, "privacy" becomes "Heimlichkeit," a word that suggests the sheltering, intimate feeling of being at home, safe from the slings and arrows of the world, from thoughtless, unfeeling, and uncaring others. It is no coincidence that the English word "home" (in German, "Heim")—a place where privacy can be enjoyed—represents a concept that simply does not exist in any of the Mediterranean languages, be they Romance, Semitic, or Turkish.

The point of this detour into cross-cultural psycholinguistics is that being alone or remaining separate from others appears to be a more desirable state in Northern European (including North American) cultures than in others. Solitude, in reasonable doses, is thought by people in these cultures to be good for the soul. We do not have to depend on comparative linguistics for evidence supporting this observation. A cross-cultural study of the ways in which people employ time throughout the day turned up the finding that Americans spend more time alone than any of the other eleven national populations studied. Germans, however, ranked closely behind Americans in the average amount of time per day they spent alone (Szalai, 1972).

In Chapter 2 we cited Altman (1975) as maintaining that attitudes toward privacy lie at the center of our concerns about territoriality and personal space. Through privacy, he says, we develop self-understanding, a knowledge of "who we are."

The cross-cultural evidence we have reviewed suggests that the motive to engage in self-exploration in order to understand ourself may be a culturally determined pattern of behavior. The facts that people in some cultures are reluctant to spend much time alone and that their languages lack adequate terms for "privacy" both suggest a disinterest in self-study. As further evidence of this tendency, we have Pollis' report that Greeks are unconcerned about the attainment of self-knowledge. She said that self-fulfillment for them is attained in terms of the demands and expectations of family and friends, one's membership group. Indeed, "the very person exists only because of these groups" (p. 32). In cultures where people are not troubled by existential doubt and where self-exploration is foreclosed, there is little need for privacy, and both territoriality and crowdedness take on quite different meanings.

Although such ideas are far out on the frontier of social ecology, some research support for them is emerging. Schmidt and his co-researchers (1976) conducted a carefully designed and elaborate survey of a random sample of some seven hundred people living in the cities of Riverside and San Bernardino in California. Anglo, black, and Chicano (mostly Mexican-American) residents were asked their reactions to a number of psychological and physical factors related to feelings of being crowded in the home, as well as in the community at large. The psychological factors included the respondents' view of crowdedness in their own homes, crowdedness experienced in shopping areas, the freedom they had to get away, and their access to privacy. The physical factors included the number of residents per room in the home and the number of automobiles the respondents had access to. In addition, the investigators assembled data relating to six other factors, including the number of people living on the respondents' census block, the distance from freeways, and the availability of parks.

After the data from the interviews had been subjected to detailed statistical analysis, a number of findings confirmed the view that members of different subcultural groups tend to hold somewhat different views on privacy, social density, and crowding, even though they are all co-participants in a common national culture. The major cross-cultural difference was that, in contrast to the Anglos, the black and Chicano residents were much more aware of their environment *outside* their immediate home—for example, their relations with their neighbors, the availability of recreational facilities, and the amount of traffic in the streets. Anglo respondents, on the other hand, were more sensitive to social density *within* the home, as measured by the number of residents per room.

The over-all picture that emerged was that the Anglos were much more oriented to home and privacy than were respondents from the other two subcultures. Differences in income to some degree affected the cross-cultural differences, but the researchers concluded that after they had adjusted their data to account for the effects of poverty or affluence, the subcultural identity of the respondents provided the best explanation for the differing patterns in their responses.

SOCIOECONOMIC FACTORS

It is always difficult in such a survey to tease out the factors that are operating to produce observable differences. Attitudes and values are not formed at one point in time but developed over long periods, from infancy onward. Although the researchers felt confident in eliminating financial status as a factor in the attitudinal differences they found, what they were really saying is that affluence or poverty had no influence at the moment they conducted their survey. Nothing in their data can tell us anything about the attitudes their respondents developed as a result of years of living in crowded, impoverished quarters or in more spacious, well-appointed homes. The greater affluence of the Anglos in the San Bernardino/ Riverside area enabled them to buy or rent living arrangements that permitted greater privacy and a lower degree of social density per room. Most of the black and Chicano people, being poorer, had to live in quarters that had a higher degree of social density per room and provided much less privacy. In other words, one explanation of these findings is that Anglos were sensitive to privacy and low density per room because they could buy it, whereas Chicanos and black people, unable to purchase these advantages, were forced to look elsewhere—out in the community—for more adequate living space. If we accept the principle that our values are based on our experiences, then it appears that the values developed by these three sets of respondents were based on the kind of lives they had been leading.

The effect of different socioeconomic environments on crowding has also been studied by Gruchow (1974), who employed the usual attitudinal and demographic dimensions and also included a physiological measure of stress: the concentration of vanillymandelic acid (VMA) in the urine of his subjects.

Gruchow found a significant relationship between VMA and the amount of crowding within the home, but only for respondents who reported that they had grown up in small families, in which they had been the only child or had only one or two siblings. Those individuals who had grown up in large families, in which there probably were more persons per room and relatively less privacy, were unaffected by the degree of crowding they experienced in their homes later as adults. In other words, crowding within the home appeared to be stressful only for those adults who had not become used to it as children. This finding recalls to mind the report by Eoyang (1974; see Ch. 2), whose survey of trailer residents at Stanford University indicated that the respondents who complained least about crowded living quarters were the ones who had grown up in larger families.

When Gruchow asked his subjects about their *perceptions* of being crowded, he got some interesting responses. The middle-class individuals' feelings of being crowded or not were totally unrelated to the actual number of persons per room in their homes. This finding suggests that as far as middle-class people are concerned, the extent to which they believe they are crowded is largely due to personal factors—personality traits and unique experiences—

than it is to social density as such. It also suggests that the statements of middle-class people about social density may not be very reliable or accurate, at least for the purposes of scientific research.

The fact that the number of people per room bore little relationship to the crowdedness reported by middle-class individuals in Gruchow's study did not mean that their perceptions were unimportant, for their excretion of VMA varied with the degree to which they felt they were being crowded. This finding lends support to the proposition we discussed in Chapter 2, namely, that it is the *perception* of crowding that seems to be important, and not such factors as the restriction of personal space and the physical event of living and working in congested quarters.

Hence we find ourselves once again up against the perplexing question of what really matters in crowding: Is it the individual's feeling that he is being crowded, or is it the restricted amount of personal space at his disposal? Neither of these views apparently tells us the whole story about crowding and whatever adverse effect it may have.

Let us examine the studies just described in search of clues that may shed some light on this problem. They tell us that social class may be one significant factor, but we suspect that experiences during infancy and childhood may be even more important.

Schmidt and his co-researchers tell us that Anglos are more sensitive to social density within the home, whereas Chicanos and blacks are more concerned about the space available to them in the community outside the home. In spite of the researchers' disclaimer, we suspect that social class does have something to do with this difference in sensitivity, because the Anglos they interviewed were mostly middle class people who probably grew up in homes in which they had more personal space and privacy at their disposal than the Chicanos and black people in their study had had. Gruchow's research confirms the relationship between early experiences and reactions to crowdedness, for those subjects who grew up in less crowded homes experienced a higher degree of stress when they were forced by circumstances to live in congested quarters as adults. There is, of course, a relationship between family size and economic status, with poor people tending to have larger families.

This brings us to the question of why people from lower socio-economic levels are inclined to be less concerned with crowdedness in living quarters. One explanation of this phenomenon may be found in the tendency of all living organisms to accommodate themselves to the stresses of the environment in which they live. This is the principle of *adaptation,* which we discussed at the end of Chapter 2. Existence would be impossible if we were unable to come to terms with and tolerate living conditions we are powerless to change. The principle of adaptation has special force during the formative years, when children not only learn to adjust to the demands of a sometimes unfriendly environment, but also come to accept its conditions as "the way things are." Thus invasions of privacy and crowding may occur so frequently that the young person not only accepts them but also feels comfortable with them and may even come to enjoy them.

This does not mean that adaptation to severe limitations of personal space does not occur at some cost. There is a price that the crowded individual must pay for having been restricted and deprived. Nor is anyone exempt, even those who grow up in more fortunate circumstances, for boundaries of time and space grow weaker and more permeable in today's world, making it more difficult to escape the problems of others. In the end, the price must be paid by all of us.

The following chapter is devoted to a discussion of the price—or, accurately, the *penalty*—paid for the crowded conditions in which at least half of the children in the world are reared.

The Social Cost
Of Crowded Homes

Chapter 4

Since its beginning as a scientific discipline, psychology has always taken a skeptical position with regard to what is called "common sense," defined variously as "what most people believe to be true," "the conventional wisdom," or "folk wisdom." Inasmuch as most people believe that crowding is a bad thing, it is not surprising that a good many psychologists report that they are unconvinced. By way of example, Jonathan Freedman (1975), maintains that crowding does not harm people, nor does it result in any kind of physical, mental, or social pathology. "People who experience high density are just as healthy, happy, and productive as those who experience lower density" (p. 7).

Freedman's conclusions are based on his interpretations of experiments with small groups, many of which he conducted, which showed that crowding produced positive effects in some instances and negative effects in others. He interpreted these results to mean that the net overall effect of crowding is a trade-off.

Although Freedman can be commended for striving to maintain a strictly objective value-free position, in keeping with scientific tradition, he does at the same time seem to have committed the fault of being overly cautious and of basing his conclusions on data that were so limited as to be irrelevant to or even misleading with respect to the larger dimensions of interpersonal and social behavior. Some psychologists criticize Freedman's neutralist state by pointing out that most of the investigations of crowding have been short-term, laboratory experiments, whose results may not be very relevant to real-life situations (McCain, Cox, and Paulus, 1976).

The fault of generalizing on limited data is not confined to research on crowding, of course. Teachers, for example, have complained for decades that the conclusions of psychologists who conduct laboratory experiments on learning bear little relationship to what actually goes on in the classroom. Part of the problem in this instance seems to be that the experimentalists, in trying to filter out factors that would becloud the results of their investigations, have eliminated some that affect the way in which a child learns in a classroom situation or whether he learns at all. Psychologists who take a broader view of the matter have noted that the values and expectations that a child brings to school, as well as those he derives from his peers, have a powerful effect on classroom learning.

Similarly, the small-scale experiments conducted by psychologists investigating crowding attempt to eliminate the effect of cultural values, early childhood experiences, and individual differences in attitudes toward close contact with others. Furthermore, such experiments are unable to tell us anything about the most crucial problem of all—the effects of crowding over long periods of time. Even the study we discussed in Chapter 2, in which men remained in crowded cells for three weeks, may tell us little about the effects of social density on people who spend months, years, or a lifetime in crowded settings. Laboratory studies do give us very specific answers to very specific questions. But so far they have not told us enough to warrant a neutral stand on crowding.

EVIDENCE OF PSYCHOPATHOLOGY

There is, as a matter of fact, a great deal of evidence to suggest that living under crowded conditions may have serious effects on human well-being. These effects are most dramatically demonstrated by studies of children growing up in different environments, whose development can be measured by such indices as the incidence of psychopathological behavior and the pace of their mental development. One such study compared the effects of living in the crowded inner city with those of life in a semirural area. The investigation consisted of a survey conducted by a team of British behavioral scientists who gathered data relating to the mental health, school performance, intelligence, family background, and home environment of ten-year-old children living in an inner London borough and on children living on the Isle of Wight, an island 147 square miles in area, located in the English Channel just off the coast of England (Rutter et al., 1975).

Their results clearly indicated that the inner London children had more difficulties than those on the Isle of Wight. For one thing, twice as many of them displayed fairly severe problems of mental health and were retarded in reading. The inner London children also averaged below national norms on a measure of nonverbal intelligence, while the Isle of Wight children scored slightly above.

In both groups there were children whose parents had a great many problems, in that they displayed neurotic or depressive symptoms, complained of marital difficulties, had been arrested, and had served time in prison. The presence of these parental problems was associated with poor mental health and retarded achievement on the part of the children, as might be expected. There were, however, considerably more problem parents and problem children in inner London than on the Isle of Wight. Children from large families in both places tended to display more problems and to be more retarded than those living in homes with fewer siblings.

After analyzing their data, the investigators concluded that the same adverse influences caused difficulties for both groups of children, but that the greater proportion of children with problems in the inner London borough could be explained in terms of the higher percentage of homes that were troubled and crowded.

The results of this comparative survey are consistent with the findings of literally hundreds of researchers who have compared inner city children with those living in other areas. Such surveys tell the same story with monotonous regularity: inner city children have more psychological problems, have lower intelligence-test scores, and are further behind in schooling. Such results emerge again and again, irrespective of the children's race or nationality.

What studies like these show is that inner city environments foster pathologies of all kinds. They create a great many problems for everyone, but especially for children. A major cause of these problems is crowding, especially within living quarters. The presence of antisocial or otherwise disturbed parents is of course an important factor, but we should keep in mind that most of these adults are themselves victims of crowding.

Poverty is often cited as a major cause of the high rate of problem behavior found in children from the inner city, but it is difficult to distinguish the effects of poverty from the other conditions ordinarily associated with it. One thing is certain, and that is that most inner-city children come from crowded homes. Living space is expensive in large cities, and the poor can afford only small, substandard quarters into which they cram their large families.

Children who grow up in the inner cities are not the only ones who suffer from the effects of crowded homes. Shapiro (1974) conducted a survey of three-year-old Israeli children living in Beersheba, a town in the Negev Desert, who were asked to carry out a number of tasks involving motor skills, like walking backwards, doing somersaults, completing jigsaw puzzles, and lacing shoes. Some tasks were essentially measures of physical development, while others required a high degree of mental competence, involving the ability to perceive accurately and form concepts.

The home background of the children was analyzed with respect to family income and the amount of crowdedness or density they experienced in their homes. Low density was designated as one or less person per room; medium density, between two or three persons per room; and high density, three or more persons per room.

Shapiro's results showed no relationship between task performance and family income, but boys from high-density homes scored significantly below boys from medium- and low-density homes in their ability to perform the assigned tasks. There was little difference between boys from medium- and low-density homes. Density apparently had little effect on girls' performance; this finding is consistent with other research studies showing that deficiencies in the home environment usually have considerably more effect on boys' development than on girls'. Boys evidently are more vulnerable.

Shapiro found some clues as to the reason that the crowdedness of the home affects children's development. The mothers in the least-crowded homes all said that they read to their children or talked with them during meals, whereas only a few of the mothers from the most crowded homes reported similar behavior. Mothers who had only a few children were able to give them more attention and to provide a more stimulating environment than those who had many children.

FAMILY SIZE AND BIRTH ORDER

Shapiro's survey is one of a handful of studies that have signaled a breakthrough for researchers seeking the basic causes underlying a number of puzzling relationships between the family environments of children and various measures of achievement. One of these puzzles is the question of why children with few siblings tend to score higher on intelligence and school achievement tests than those coming from larger families. This relationship between family size and test scores did not attract much attention at first, because it was thought that it was merely an expression of the difference between socioeconomic status. In contrast to blue-collar or working-class parents, middle-class parents tend to be better educated, to have higher income, and to beget fewer children. The fact that their more-advantaged children scored higher than less-advantaged ones was not considered very surprising.

A study conducted by Belmont and Marolla (1973), however, was able to demonstrate that family size has an effect over and beyond any that might be attributed to its socioeconomic status.

Their research consisted of an analysis of the family backgrounds of some four hundred thousand Dutch draftees who had taken a standardized intelligence test as part of their induction procedures. Their finding that draftees from larger families tended to have lower intelligence test scores than those from smaller ones was consistent with previous research, but they also found that this tendency persisted even when the socioeconomic status of the parents was controlled. In other words, young men from middle-class homes who had many siblings scored lower than those from small middle-class families, while the sons of working-class parents who had few children scored higher than those whose working-class parents had many children.

Another intriguing finding reported by Belmont and Marolla was that the birth order of the draftees also had a significant influence on their intelligence test scores. The earlier the young man had appeared in the birth-order sequence in his family, the higher his score. In other words, firstborns tended to have the highest scores, those born second the next highest, and so forth. The only exception to this trend was the only child, who scored slightly below the second-born sons of families of two or three children, but about the same as the firstborns in families of four, and ahead of the firstborns of families of five or more children. This birth-order effect appeared at all social and economic levels and was consistent with the relationship between birth order and intelligence and school success observed by a number of other researchers over the last five decades.

What was especially significant about the Dutch study, however, was that the huge numbers of subjects drawn from all social and economic levels confirmed beyond a reasonable doubt that large families tend to have a depressing effect on mental development and that children appearing later in the birth-order sequence are at a disadvantage where mental development is concerned.

The question of *why* family size and birth order both influence mental development was up to that point largely unresolved, although a number of theories had been proposed to explain the two effects as separate phenomena. It remained for Robert B.

Zajonc (1976), a psychologist at the University of Michigan, to propose a single theory that explained both effects. His "confluence theory" states that the more children there are, the smaller are the shares of the family pool of intellectual resources that are available to each of them, and the less adequate their mental development. Hence they score lower on measures of mental development, like tests of intelligence and reading ability.

The theory also explains why birth order is important. When the firstborn arrives, he has the family's intellectual resources all to himself during the crucial first two years of development. With the arrival of the second child, the firstborn loses some of his share, but he is already off to a good start. Each succeeding child, therefore, gets a smaller and smaller share of the family's intellectual resources.

Zajonc points out that lengthening the time intervals between children can compensate for some of these negative effects. An infant requires a great deal of time and attention. A child who is, say, four or five years old is able to shift for himself with less need for care and attention than is a child who is only 18 or 24 months older than the newborn. When siblings appear closer together, each one gets less of the attention he needs for optimal intellectual development.

Another positive aspect to longer time spacing between children is that it enables children to learn more from one another. Older siblings teach younger ones games, warn them about behavior that will get them into trouble, help them interpret the parental demands, and the like. A two-year-old can learn more from a five-year-old than he can from a sibling who is only four. Conversely, a five-year-old is likely to get more out of teaching a two-year-old than a four-year-old can.

This last is important, because teaching others is an excellent way of developing one's own reasoning powers. As Zajonc says, "One who has to explain something will see from the other's reactions whether the explanation was understood, and be prompted to improve the explanation, with the consequence that his or her own understanding of the matter is improved" (p. 231). One of the reasons that only children do not score quite so high as firstborns in families of two children or more is that they have no siblings to teach, according to Zajonc.

The briefest time span between births occurs with twins, of course. Inasmuch as parents have only so much time to devote to infant care, it follows that each member of a pair of infant twins would get less attention than a single infant would during this crucial stage of development. If Zajonc's theory about the division of family intellectual resources is valid, we would therefore expect that twins would score lower on intelligence tests than other children. Results reported in a number of studies confirm this expectation. Twins taking college aptitude tests, for example, score lower than only children, first-borns, second-borns, and third-borns. We should also expect that in instances in which one of a pair of twins was stillborn, or died in early infancy, the surviving twin would develop more normally, like any other singly born child. Once again, the data confirm this prediction. A comparison of intelligence test results indicates that twins whose co-twin died early scored higher than did twins who both survived.

Zajonc's theory also provides an explanation for another phenomenon that has been puzzling educators, parents, and behavioral scientists: the decline in college aptitude scores over the past 15 years. His analysis of the cause of declining college entrance test scores is ingenious. He points out that the highest average scores were obtained by high school graduates in 1962-63, who had been born in 1945, when the birth rate was low, and there were relatively few children per family. After 1945 family size increased, and after 1962, college aptitude test scores declined. In other words, the decline in scores that has been puzzling us was due to the fact that high school graduates were coming from increasingly larger families. Zajonc states that the bottom of the decline should be reached in 1980, when children born in 1962, the year in which American families reached their largest average size, will attain the age of 18 and become eligible to take tests whose scores will admit them to college.

Zajonc's theory is supported by the fact that test scores made by elementary school children in recent years have been rising. These increases reflect the greater competence of children born after 1962, when the average American family began to become smaller once more. The fact that these children have had fewer siblings means that they had proportionately larger shares of the intellectual resources of their families. In 1987, according to Zajonc, college aptitude scores should be back where they were in 1962.

Zajonc introduced other data to support his conclusions about the relationship between intellectual development on the one hand and family size and sibling spacing on the other. An analysis of scores made on reading comprehension tests administered to ten-year-old children in 13 countries indicates that the best performance was found in countries with low birth rates, whereas countries with high birth rates reported poorer performance. Similarly, a survey of family size and IQ conducted in France indicated that in provinces where families tended to be larger the children had lower IQs, whereas the highest IQs were found in areas where family sizes were smaller.

Although Zajonc did not specifically mention crowdedness in his report, his theory clearly implicates it as an important factor in the intellectual development of children. Indeed, his analysis neatly dovetails with the results of surveys like the ones we discussed earlier—the comparison between the children in the inner London borough and on the Isle of Wight and the study of social density in Israeli homes.

The fact that a child's intellectual development is related to his share of the psychological resources of his family does not mean that other factors are irrelevant. Although crowding reduces the amount of parental attention a child can claim, it produces other effects which can have an inhibiting or depressing effect on intellectual growth, as well as on other aspects of his development. The research we have discussed in the foregoing chapters supported two key points: first, that crowdedness increases violations of personal space and thus reduces privacy; and second, that individuals can adapt themselves to life under such conditions. The fact that adults in our culture vary in their attitudes and feelings about personal space suggests that they may have experienced different degrees of crowdedness during childhood. The cross-cultural research we reported also suggests that differing values with respect to family size are correlated with attitudes about privacy. Southern Europeans, who are relatively unconcerned about privacy, have historically had higher birth rates and larger families than Northern Europeans, who are much more concerned about privacy. Studies of attitudes toward privacy have not been conducted in Southern Asia, Africa, and Latin America, where women are ordinarily expected to bear six children, but one would expect it to possess a low value and even be derogated.

What is life like in a family of, say, two parents and six children living in moderate-to-poor circumstances? In such families, children share beds and baths, do their homework together, and are very seldom alone. This is communal living with a vengeance, for there is little territoriality. Assets—food, toys, living space, and parental attention—are held in common, and the boundaries of personal space are very restricted and are often violated. Chaos and anarchy in such families are likely to be held in check by parental strictness; in cultures where large families prevail, authoritarian and traditional values dominate. Personal freedom and self-determination are suppressed, for fear that stronger or cleverer individuals will exploit the others in the group and thus receive more than their fair share of the limited assets that are available.

Crowded homes are rich in stimulation. Babies cry, parents scold, children run in and out, radios or television sets play constantly. If the dwelling is located in a city or suburban slum, there is also noise from the street and from the neighbors. Psychological research shows that a certain amount of stimulation is a good thing, for it arouses the human organism, helps focus attention, and facilitates thinking. But an overabundance of stimulation inhibits intellectual activities, especially when prolonged. Under conditions of overstimulation, the organism reacts defensively. Neural mechanisms block out sensory input and prevent it from reaching the attending, acting, and thinking areas of the brain. Prolonged overstimulation leads to insensitivity and apathy, the characteristic responses to adaptation, especially when the stimulation lacks order and is unpredictable, as it often is in crowded settings.

What stimulation produces in the human organism is arousal. Arousal may also result from involvement in a demanding task, like putting together a complex puzzle, working a mathematical problem, or delivering a speech before an audience. Psychological research shows that there is a negative relationship between the amount of stimulation we are subjected to and the complexity of the task we are able to perform. A large amount of stimulation may actually help with simple tasks; this is why peeling potatoes and other routine household chores go better when we listen to lively music. But many people find music distracting if they are working at a more intellectually demanding task, such as the preparation of income tax forms.

The research on crowding is consistent with these observations. In one set of experiments, students were required to solve fairly difficult problems involving mazes which were concealed from view. Results showed that increasing the size of the group, decreasing the size of the room, and decreasing the distance among the subjects produced poorer performances (Paulus et al., 1976). Complex tasks are best performed alone, but the performance of simple tasks can be enhanced by the presence of others (Hunt and Hillery, 1973). Even some crowding may over brief periods of time make for a better performance with simple, well-learned tasks (Hillery and Fugita, 1975).

When we are working at tasks, the presence of others may be distracting. Again, distraction seems to aid in the performance of simple tasks but to interfere with more complex ones (Sanders and Baron, 1975).

Let us pull these research findings all together and see what light they shed on the intellectual development of small children. About the time the child acquires the rudiments of language, he starts to learn ways of coping with the world in symbolic terms. Instead of grabbing for a cookie and getting his hand slapped, he learns to use language to ask for it. He listens to his mother's directions and is able to carry out orders and avoid trouble. He is able to play games because he has learned the rules that govern them.

Countless episodes in a child's everyday life require him to give his attention to some aspect of his environment, analyze it, and decide what action to take. Adults engage in such activities a hundred times a day, casually, without giving any special thought to what they are doing. But children have to work much harder at the task of understanding what is going on around them, if they are to succeed in coping satisfactorily.

A child who grows up in a crowded family will have greater difficulty in dealing with the more complex problems that life poses. Solving such problems requires attention and concentration, and life in a crowded family is more likely to be distracting, partly because the noise level is higher, but also because there are more invasions of personal space than in smaller family homes. It is hard to figure out what Mother means when she says, "Watch out for your little brother," or "No, that's not good for you," at a moment when your brothers and sisters are jostling you.

A child's success in learning to get along with others requires a considerable degree of empathy, the ability to determine how others think and feel. But it is virtually impossible to learn to empathize in a crowded home. For one thing, which one of the family do you start to empathize with? And with whom do you empathize when several people are demanding your attention simultaneously?

Learning to empathize in crowded, confused situations is difficult enough for an adult, but it is much harder for a child. Although old saws like "As the twig is bent . . ." suggest that children are more flexible than adults, in actuality they are inclined to be quite rigid and conservative. Eleanor E. Maccoby (1975) describes the typical preschool child as liking to have all the furniture in the same place, his food served in the same dishes, and the members of the family in their same places at mealtime. When his physical and social environment has some degree of order and predictibility, he is able to concentrate on understanding one or two crucial events. She recommends that parents try to help children's mental development by arranging a stable and predictable environment, in which not too many elements change at once.

Maccoby's views about orderliness and stability in children's home environments are supported by a number of research studies. Bradley and Caldwell (1976) rated the home environment of six-month-old infants on a number of factors, including one they termed "organization of physical and temporal environment." Homes rating high on this factor were ones in which objects such as furniture, utensils, and toys had definite locations and in which family activities such as meals, bedtime, and baths occurred according to some predictable schedule. Homes rating low were ones that were untidy and messy, in which clothing was dropped on the floor or on nearby furniture when it was changed, and in which meals and other daily events occurred haphazardly.

When Bradley and Caldwell administered intelligence tests to the children four years later, they found that children from homes in which organization and scheduling were present had significantly higher IQs than did children from disorganized and chaotic homes.

Another research team studied black fifth-graders from economically disadvantaged homes in the Central Harlem area of New York City. The investigators examined the school records of the children and identified those who had scored significantly higher than the national average of standardized tests of reading and arithmetic. This group of high achievers was compared with a second group who had been scoring far below average on the same tests. The homes of the children were then visited and evaluated by a black social worker. She found that 90 percent of the homes of the high-achieving children could be described as clean, neat, and orderly, in contrast to only 62 percent of those of the low achievers (Greenberg and Davidson, 1972).

Two comments can be made about the relationship between crowding and the organization of time and space in the home. One is that the more crowded the home, the more difficult it is to keep things organized. Family members continually forget to put things where they belong, frequently demand to be exempted from tidying up, and create emergencies that require drastic changes in the physical environment of the home. Many a distracted and exhausted parent despairs of maintaining order or keeping to some kind of a schedule and surrenders to chaos.

The second comment is that many of the negative features of crowded homes can be kept at a minimum when parents doggedly insist on maintaining some kind of order. Exceptions are made for emergencies, of course, but when the emergency is over, the rule is "back to the schedule." This course of action takes great resolution and determination on the part of the parents and requires that they behave at times in authoritarian and arbitrary ways. What we are describing is, in essence, enforced territoriality.

In an orderly home, everyone has his place, his possessions, and his assigned duties. Because everyone knows what is his and what he is supposed to do, and also knows what belongs to others and what they are supposed to do, life is predictable, and the distractions resulting from invasion of personal space and privacy are kept under control. In such an environment, children are able to concentrate on the important task of learning to understand and cope with their physical and social environment. The mental and physical development of children requires more than order, of course, but it does seem to be an important factor, as the studies we have described indicate.

Is there any antidote to the crowded home? Is there any way in which society can help children whose mental development has been impeded or inhibited by having to cope with the chaos and distraction of what psychologists term "a perceptual overload"?

INTERVENTION

An obvious antidote is that of getting the children out of the crowded home into a less crowded environment in which there is order, predictability, and the opportunity to concentrate on mental and physical tasks they would otherwise have difficulty in mastering. One experimental attempt to create such an environment is the

Early Training Program of the George Peabody College for Teachers in Nashville, Tennessee (Gray and Klaus, 1970). Black children from large and impoverished families attended a summer preschool program, in which there was one adult for every five children. The children received a great deal of individual attention and were encouraged and liberally rewarded for attempting such simple tasks as throwing a ball into a wastebasket, planning and carrying out small projects, and putting away toys after play. During the months when the preschool was not in session, an assistant made monthly visits to the children's homes and encouraged their mothers to carry on the kinds of activities the children had been engaged in at school.

Intelligence tests given at various intervals indicated that the participating children made somewhat higher gains in IQ than comparable groups of children who had not been exposed to the program. After the children had left the program and had been in elementary school a few years, however, their advantage faded and their IQs declined to about what they would have been had they not been involved in the special program.

The Early Training Program served as a model for Operation Head Start, which has brought some form of fairly individualized preschool experience to millions of deprived children over the last dozen years. The details of the controversy of the past few years over the efficacy of Head Start are beyond the scope of this discussion, but suffice it to say that its results, as measured by intelligence tests, are similar to those of the Early Training Program. Where Head Start children made superior gains in intelligence test scores, the advantage generally faded within a year of two of their entrance into grade school.

When we look at these programs in terms of the probable effects of overcrowding, they seem to be examples of "too little and too late." Children do not begin preschool training until they are three years of age. By then they have been exposed to three years of overcrowded conditions and have developed ineffective and nonproductive habits of thinking and behaving. Furthermore, they spend only a few hours a day in the special programs and then return to their crowded homes. In only a few programs is there the carefully planned procedure of home visitation developed in the George Peabody program, whereby mothers are encouraged to work with the children and thus mitigate some of the unfortunate outcomes of crowding and other aspects of social and economic deprivation.

This is not to say that intervention programs like Operation Head Start are without social value. Anything that expands the intellectual and social horizons of children is worthwhile. But it is too much to expect that so minimal an experience can undo the deleterious effects of early crowding.

By far the most successful of the "early intervention programs" is the one conducted in Milwaukee by Garber and Heber (1975), who worked with black inner-city children and their mothers. The mothers of these children averaged some 25 IQ points below the norm. What usually happens to such children is that they eventually end up at intellectual levels similar to that of their mothers or, in any event, well below average.

Children entered the Milwaukee early intervention program when they were only three months old. They received individual care and attention eight hours a day from a trained staff who took special pains to get the children involved in dealing with problems and tasks appropriate to their stage of maturity. The ratio between adults and children ensured the maximum in attention, for it varied between one to two children per adult. The experience of these children was, in short, totally different from that of the child who grows up in a typical crowded inner-city home. A supplemental program was also initiated to prepare the children's mothers for employment in semiskilled jobs.

The results of the program, as indicated by intelligence tests administered at the end of five years, were quite dramatic. Children who had participated in the special program had an average IQ of almost 130, far above the IQ of 90 that was the average of a comparison group of children from the same kind of homes. There is little doubt that the special training provided by the investigators' assistants had some effect on these results, but we should also recognize that the children were away from their crowded homes eight hours a day from infancy onward.

Another study indicates that special training is not essential to overcome the effects of crowdedness on children. Wayne Dennis (1973) followed the development of children in an orphanage in Beirut, Lebanon. The institution was staffed by five nuns who attempted to care for the needs of a hundred or more infants and toddlers, crowded into totally inadequate quarters. Apathy and depression were the characteristic responses of the children, and their average IQ was 52, which Dennis said was the lowest ever obtained for any group of otherwise normal children.

Adoptive parents provided the only means of salvation from this crowded setting. Dennis' follow-up studies indicated that once children had been adopted, their mental development began to accelerate. The earlier in life the children were adopted, the more nearly normal was their intellectual development, thus showing how important it is for children to escape from crowded conditions during their first few months.

We have focused on the effects of crowding on mental development because it can be measured easily and reliably and hence makes a clear-cut case against crowding. It is, furthermore, a key factor in the ability to cope with the problems posed by a society that grows every day more complex.

MENTAL HEALTH

What affects one area of human development influences other aspects as well, of course. The crowding that during early childhood inhibits mental growth also has negative effects on mental health. At the start of this chapter, we noted that children from a crowded inner London borough displayed more emotional problems than did children living on the Isle of Wight. In contrast to the parents of the Isle of Wight children, the inner-London parents also displayed more problems of adjustment. They, like their children, tended to be products of a crowded environment.

Although people who grow up in crowded settings appear to accommodate themselves to social density, there are certain experiences characteristic of such an environment that are bound to cause difficulties, no matter how philosophical and accepting one's attitudes may be. The person growing up in such an environment may never miss privacy but may still pay a price in terms of personal and social adjustment.

As we noted in Chapter 2, privacy is essential for self-evaluation, that is, for self-examination and analysis of one's relations with others. It is impossible to engage in the necessary contemplation or self-exploration in a crowded environment in which one must be constantly attending to and coping with the actions, demands, expectations, announcements, and pronouncements of others. People who grow up and live in situations that lack privacy are therefore likely to lack the psychological resources to deal with problems of interpersonal conflict.

Without privacy, we are unable to develop an adequate understanding of ourselves and others. As a consequence, our relations with other people are likely to lack depth and to be impulsive or ritualistic—unthinking, in other words. In the everyday course of events, this lack of depth may not be apparent, but in time of crisis, people tend to react either with panic or with apathy. Indeed, much of the aggressiveness that characterizes inner-city life is essentially a frightened response to frustration or a relatively minor disturbance on the part of people who have never experienced privacy and hence are without inner resources.

As mental health is more difficult to measure than intellectual development, data showing the effect of crowding on personal and social adjustment are not easily obtained. There are, nevertheless, a few studies that indicate a direct relationship between social density and emotional problems. Gary W. Evans (1975) observed that subjects who had been subjected to crowding in an experiment displayed less ability to tolerate frustration and were less able to cooperate afterwards than did subjects who had been in a normal or control situation. An analysis of the data indicated, furthermore, that these effects were general and not more characteristic of one type of personality than another.

What problems of adjustment emerge when individuals experience crowding over long periods of time in real-life situations? This question was addressed by a team of behavioral scientists who studied the reactions of prison inmates to various degrees of social density (McCain et al., 1976). The investigators used an indirect measure of psychological adjustment often employed by clinical psychologists, the number of illness complaints over and beyond those associated with infections, fractures, contusions, or the like. The most frequent categories of the complaints they tallied were back pain, nausea, skin rash, sinusitis, constipation, chest pains, and asthma. Such complaints generally involve social or emotional stress and are often designated as "psychosomatic symptoms."

Some of the prisoners were confined to one-man or two-man cells, whereas others had been assigned to dormitories housing 26 or more inmates. The investigators compared inmates in the two types of housing with respect to the number of requests they made for medical treatment of psychosomatic symptoms. The illness complaint rate was much higher among dormitory residents who of course had much more exposure to invasions of personal space and other kinds of crowding experiences. Similar findings emerged from a five-week survey of prisoners in county jail, where crowding was more intense. When inmates were classified into two groups according to the crowdedness they experienced, those who were exposed to the highest degree of social density made considerably more formal requests for medical treatment than did those assigned to less crowded quarters. Indeed, during the latter weeks of the survey, inmates living in crowded quarters generated twice as many illness complaints as did those exposed to a lower degree of social density.

The fact that psychosomatic symptoms of the type tallied in these surveys possess psychological overtones does not mean that they do not involve physical stress. There is little doubt that crowded conditions produce measurable degrees of physical stress.

Evans (1975) found that subjects exposed to crowding showed increases in blood pressure and heart rate. Similarly, a study of the effect of crowding on inmates of three correctional institutions found that prisoners living in dormitories had higher blood pressure and faster heart rates than those in one-man and two-man cells (D'Atri, 1974).

These studies show that crowding takes its toll in the form of an elevated degree of physical arousal or stress. Hence it is not surprising that stress-related symptoms, like back pains and asthma, would increase. Under conditions of crowdedness, the entire human organism suffers: Mental development is inhibited, self-insight and understanding are made difficult or impossible, interpersonal relations are impaired, physical symptoms of stress appear, and mental health problems are increased.

In the following chapter we shall explore some of the ways in which the crowded urban environment contributes to and aggravates these and other difficulties.

Urban Stress

Chapter 5

Nations, governments, politics, and religions—all rest on the basic phenomenon of human existence, the city.—Oswald Spengler

God the first garden made, and the first city Cain.—Abraham Cowley

Cities—breeding places of culture and crime, magnificence and misery, the sublime and the sleazy—have been celebrated and cursed ever since they emerged as the wellsprings of civilization almost six millennia ago. After hundreds of thousands of years of roaming, human beings began settling down, creating cities or quasicities first in the Mesopotamian river basin (in today's Iraq) and later, either by invention or diffusion, in the valleys of the Nile, Indus, and Yellow rivers; along the shores of the Mediterranean; in West Africa; and in middle America and the Andes of South America. Over the centuries many great civilizations, and the cities that were their pinnacles, flourished for a time, then floundered or perished as empires dissolved and a depleted countryside no longer could cater to urban demands. The ruins of centers that once were the habitats of kings, seats of learning, and nuclei of innovation are bleak reminders of ephemeral glory. Some of the ancient cities have endured, and any city in the United States is an upstart by comparison.

Populous cities are another matter, a modern phenomenon with incalculable social and economic consequences. In the few urbanized societies in the preindustrial past, cities rarely contained over 100,000 inhabitants, and only occasionally as many as 30,000; a population of 10,000 or even 5,000 was more usual. In fact, compared with the modern metropolis, most of these centers were veritable villages, scarcely to be dignified as cities. Even as late as 1850, only about 2 percent of the world's people lived in cities of over 100,000 inhabitants; now 24 percent do; and an estimated 40 percent will do so by the year 2000 (Davis, 1972). At the beginning of this century, only 11 cities had passed the million mark. By 1950 there were 75 such cities. Now there are 191, with 101 of them in the developing nations.

But these figures don't convey the full measure of the recent momentum of the urban revolution, for cities aren't stopping at the million mark. In 1950 there were only two cities crammed with some 10 million people, New York and London. By 1970 four such urban giants existed, and projections indicate that by 1985 there will be no fewer than 17. Tokyo, it is predicted, will contain roughly 25 million. Surrealist scenarios for the not-too-distant future have Calcutta and Bombay, hardly model cities today, teeming with 100 million inhabitants (Ward, 1976, p. 4).

A few decades ago, Gertrude Stein observed that in the United States "there is more space where nobody is than where anybody is. That is what makes America what it is." Her words are even more germane today, for about 75 percent of our population have opted, or felt compelled, to bunch together on a mere 1.5 percent of America's vast expanse. It is predicted that this metropolitan population will climb to 85 percent by the end of the century. New York, which in 1970 already had 26,343 residents per square mile, will reportedly bulge with 25 million souls (Pickard, 1972). (The Indians who sold Manhattan to the colonists for $24 worth of trinkets and a bottle of whiskey were, according to some critics of

New York, blessed with a long view that no modern predictions, however computerized, can match.)

The snag in all current cystal gazing is that, as Albert Mayer (1967) points out in *The Urgent Future,* "trend is not destiny." The world by the year 2000 very possibly will have more urban dwellers than rural people, but no one can predict what political, social, and technological changes will intervene to transform the course of world-wide urbanization. How long can cities continue to grow by chance rather than by design, denying millions of their inhabitants such minimal provisions as a roof over their heads, sewage systems, and piped water?

Even now in the United States, whose urban population for the most part fares considerably better than do its counterparts in Latin America, Asia, and Africa, anti-urbanism, always smoldering, has erupted with unusual force. More and more Americans appear to be echoing the sentiment of Thomas Jefferson: "I view great American cities as pestilential to the morals, health, and the liberties of man." Or, in contemporary terms, the big city is slick but sick. U.S. public-opinion polls over the years have consistently demonstrated that the majority of people living in big cities would prefer to live in smaller ones. The malaise of urban life has recently become so acute that Americans are now reversing a fifty year trend: they are moving out, not just from the center city but from the entire metropolitan area (*U.S. News & World Report,* April 5, 1976).

While this exodus may be just a trickle, it is significant because it has hit even those cities generally regarded as eminently civilized. Not long ago Arthur Louis (1976, p. 67) made a study of 50 of the nation's largest cities to determine which one was the worst. As he puts it, "I'd like to believe that it doesn't require any perversity of character to go looking for the worst city. There *are* no good cities in America today—only bad and less bad." The concluded survey put Newark at the bottom of the list, with no serious challenger in sight. The choicest spot in the nation turned out to be Seattle, an urban gem frequently noted for its livability. Yet in late 1976 Seattle began running TV ads to urge its residents to stay put. The commercials were aimed particularly at middle-income families, a notable number of whom were fleeing to the suburbs in search of better schools, a lower crime rate, and larger houses at a lower cost. Like many another American city, Seattle was gradually becoming a city of the elderly, of young, unmarried professionals, and the poor and unemployed. Carried to extremes, the exodus of middle-income groups could result in cities inhabited primarily by the very rich and the very poor.

Whatever the rank of the 50 cities surveyed by Louis or of any other city in the world, each holds out the basic promise of economic opportunity (which sometimes turns out to be a trap). Each has a special ambiance, compounded not only of its physical appearance but also of its history, legends, and cultural traditions. The environs, the pattern (or lack of one), the architecture, the tempo and pace, the composition and density of population, and the amenities of cities vary so widely that any city on earth arouses a vast range of emotions and sentiments, from the highly romantic to the downright pathological (Strauss, 1961 and 1968; Terkel, 1967; Lynch, 1960; Fischer, 1976). Almost any adjective in the dictionary could be and probably has been used to describe cities in general or in particular. Any argument in favor of a city can be countered by an argument against it. Cities by their very nature provoke audacious and controversial declarations. They are not experienced in the same way by different individuals or by different groups.

Back in 1843 the British industrial revolution produced a rather extraordinary publication, *A Gazetteer of Disgusting Places*. Chances are that its compilers experienced some ambivalence despite the document's theme, recognizing that places can be both vile and beautiful, terrifying and enticing, hateful and lovable (Briggs, 1968). The rush, the swarm, the cacophony of big cities is appalling to some, appealing to others. Cities have ever drawn those seeking opportunity—or oblivion. Certainly not the least of their attractions is that they provide a haven for malcontents, misfits, and "unusual" people, offering not just a wide range of freedom but also the aid and comfort of like associates. Although the small community, as Robert Park (1969, p. 91) once noted, merely tolerates eccentricity, the city rewards it.

Tourists may come away with a broad if superficial knowledge of a city, aware of immense areas that remain completely unknown to many of its residents. The visitors' perceptions are colored in large part, however, by their preconceptions. For instance, a tourist in New York will tend to see what he or she *expects* to see—and nowadays that means a frenetic, violent place inhabited by millions of cold-hearted bastards. Standards of comparison also strongly influence the tourists' view. A New Yorker visiting Rome might regard the pace as leisurely, whereas a visitor from Santa Rosa, California, might consider it hectic. Still, no psychological or sociological studies, however well-intentioned or "objective," are likely to convince people that they're misguided if they find, say, Detroit alarming and Zurich charming.

Innumerable scholarly treatises have indicated (although far from conclusively) that the prevalent negative attitude toward cities isn't necessarily well founded. But people tend to rely on their gut feelings. And, rightly or wrongly, the image of the city—at least the American city—today is not so much one of vibrancy, diversity, and possibilities as one of fear, filth, and frustration. The attempt to understand the pathology of American cities has spawned a host of contradictory theories and statistics. Is the city the agent of or a haven for pathological behavior, squalor, discord? In pondering this dilemma, Hubert Humphrey (1968, p. 6) writes: "I have often wondered whether the obsolescence and deterioration of our cities reflect what has happened to people in our culture or whether the deterioration of our cities has resulted in the deterioration and the deprivation of the human spirit."

Human beings have an astonishing ability to adjust, biologically and socially, to seemingly undesirable living conditions. While the initial effects of this adaptation may not be particularly bad, the insidious secondary ones may be highly detrimental both to the individual and to society. The passive acceptance of such conditions as crowding, polluted environments, competitive behavior, and endless vulgarity can eventually lead to physical degradation and emotional atrophy, to personal and social degeneration. As René Dubos (1965, p. 279) eloquently expresses it:

> Life in the modern city has become a symbol of the fact that man can become adapted to starless skies, treeless avenues, shapeless buildings, tasteless bread, joyless celebrations, spiritless pleasures—to a life without reverence for the past, love for the present, or hope for the future.

As populations build up, stress inevitably does too. The human propensity for adaptation notwithstanding, the ability to handle stress gradually begins to diminish. The demographic yardsticks that sociologists use to analyze urban life—numbers, density, and heterogeneity—inevitably leave out a basic psychological component, that is, the ways in which individuals experience city life. People can suffer from both sensory deprivation and stimulus-information overload. An excess of either can be destructive. One of the magnets of cities is the ceaseless stimulation they offer. But how much stimulation is too much?

INPUT OVERLOAD

When stimuli—the actions and impositions of others as well as sounds and sights and smells—become too profuse or too varied, individuals are impelled to deal with input overload. The concept of input overload (also called sensory, psychic, stimulus, or cognitive overload) is far from new. Some 75 years ago the German philosopher and sociologist Georg Simmel tackled the subject, and its increasing pertinence has recently made it the pivot of numerous sociological studies (Simmel, 1950; Milgram, 1970; Meier, 1962; Miller, 1961). But one of the most evocative descriptions of the impact of an overloaded environment appears in Renata Adler's novel *Speedboat* (1976, p. 3):

> Speech, tennis, music, skiing, manners, love. . . . You've caught the rhythm of them once and for all, in your sleep at night. The city,

of course, can wreck it. So much insomnia. So many rhythms collide. The salesgirl, the landlord, the guests, the bystanders, sixteen varieties of social circumstances in a day. Everyone has the power to call your whole life into question here. Too many people have access to your state of mind.

Unable to scan, let alone process, all the stimulus-information, people develop tactics to divert the excessive inputs, often without being aware that they are doing so. In order to protect themselves from too many demands, they come up with adaptive responses that simplify the information they are intermittently bombarded with. This can result however in a loss of life-enhancing stimuli. The individual may become withdrawn and somewhat callous, enmeshed in a stultified, routinized existence allowing only super-ficial relationships and geared toward anonymity.

Architect Christopher Alexander (1967, p. 84) calls this "the autonomy-withdrawal syndrome." "Stress," he says, "forces people to withdraw into themselves; autonomy allows them to. Pushed by stress, pulled by autonomy, people have withdrawn into a private world where they believe that they are self-sufficient." Eventually self-sufficiency becomes an ideal, making "intimate contact seem less necessary, and . . . more and more difficult to achieve in practice." It is not, then, stress as such that is to blame for the ills of city life, but rather the means used to try to escape it.

The adaptive responses to overload are largely responsible for the often-castigated behavior of the city dweller. Because these escape hatches are sometimes used unconsciously, an urbanite may denounce other urbanites for their lack of compassion, not realizing that he or she, by using the same response to ward off stress, may appear to be equally unfeeling.

Of the many forms of adaptive response, social psychologist Stanley Milgram (1970, p. 1462) has noted six in particular:

1. Less time is allotted to each input (which contributes to the "brusque" quality of city life).
2. Lower-priority inputs are screened out. (The urbanite steers clear of the drunk—or presumed drunk—who inelegantly takes up side-walk space.)

3. In numerous situations one party shifts responsibility to another. ("That's *your* problem"; "It's none of my business.")

4. Personal contact is discouraged. (Phone numbers are increasingly unlisted, and receivers are often left off the hook to stop incoming calls; assuming a frosty demeanor is also highly effective, as is the lofty "Talk to my secretary.")

5. Various filtering devices lessen the intensity of inputs, thus keeping involvements at an anemic level. (Insulation from distractions allows traditional courtesies to be disregarded.)

6. Specialized institutions serve as a sponge for the inputs that would otherwise deluge the individual. (Welfare agencies provide funds for the poor, who might otherwise become beggars and hound pedestrians.) While this buffer role of institutions cushions the individual, it unfortunately also estranges him or her from the social environment.

Frequently lacking direct contact and integration with the surrounding world, the city dweller tends to become indifferent, blasé, alienated. As human relationships are eroded by depersonalization, social responsibility plummets. In Milgram's view (1970, p. 1462),

The ultimate adaptation to an overloaded social environment is to totally disregard the needs, interests, and demands of those whom one does not define as relevant to the satisfaction of personal needs, and to develop highly efficient perceptual means of determining whether an individual falls into the category of friend or stranger.

This is not to suggest, however, that the urban milieu creates some monstrous change in an individual's personality or in the basic ways he or she interacts with others. Lyn Lofland (1973, p. 178) has concluded from a study of encounters between strangers in public places that the urbanite "did not lose the capacity for knowing others personally. But he gained the capacity for knowing others only categorically. [He] did not lose the capacity for the deep, long-lasting, multifaceted relationship. But he gained the capacity for the surface, fleeting, restricted relationship." Alternative explanation is that people are more likely to be warm and open with, and less likely to exploit, those who share their subculture than those whose subculture is decidedly different. It is the situation, rather than the intrinsic personalities of the people, that sets the tone of these human interactions.

Yet it is all too easy to point to personality deficiencies—cowardliness, selfishness, Machiavellianism, sadism, alienation (the list is endless)—as the root cause of the failure of strangers to assist someone in trouble. If this simplistic explanation is untenable, what accounts for the well-documented phenomenon of so-called bystander apathy?

BYSTANDER INTERVENTION

"I don't want to get involved." This is just common sense in some circumstances, but during emergencies it can have tragic consequences. The most notorious example of such a tragedy was the murder of Kitty Genovese in Kew Gardens, New York City, in 1964. Returning home from a night job around 3:00 A.M., Ms. Genovese was set upon by a still-unknown assailant and repeatedly stabbed for more than half an hour. At least 38 neighbors heard her screams, went to their windows, and observed the attack. Yet not one tried to help her. Not one even phoned the police, until she was dead.

Aided by the enormous publicity given the episode by the mass media, by savants and pseudo-savants, the public at large saw the slaying as a blatant example of the gross inhumanity bred by city life. In the ensuing years newspaper stories of similar cases have proliferated. In 1964 the Genovese murder shocked the nation. By 1976 such sordid events were almost routinely reported. For example, in late 1976, in Daly City, California, a man was murdered in the parking lot of a hamburger joint. On hearing the ruckus outside, the customers in the restaurant went to see what was going on, some of them calmly munching their hamburgers while watching the man die. No one went to his aid. The story barely made the headlines.

Is the Good Samaritan obsolete? Has all the slaughter on TV made a real event just another "entertainment"? Mesmerized by mayhem, have people sunk into a collective inertia?

Violence aside, what happens if someone just passes out on the sidewalk? Does anybody care? A few days before Christmas of 1976, Joseph Torchia, a reporter for the *San Francisco Examiner,* conducted an experiment to see if anyone did care. Dressed in Levis and a suede jacket (he didn't look like a bum), he spent from mid-morning to mid-afternoon either collapsing in front of people or simply lying on the sidewalk. He did this in four disparate districts of San Francisco—the seedy Tenderloin, the hang-loose North Beach, the Financial District, and a small shopping area of the largely residential Sunset District. Only in North Beach was he immediately offered assistance. In the three other areas he was ignored (in one case by at least 50 passers-by), stepped over, and even kicked before someone tried to help him (Torchia, 1976).

Around the same time a woman sitting in a half-filled subway car in New York City was approached by a stranger who grabbed a notebook she was carrying and proceeded to tear up the pages. When she struggled to get the notebook back, the man scratched her face, then relinquished what was left of the notebook. The rest of the people in the car just sat and watched; some of them laughed. The woman was the wife of Chayym Zeldis, a novelist and poet. Pondering his wife's experience but even more the apparent coldheartedness exhibited in far worse circumstances, Zeldis (1976) writes: "We have sounded the depth of the oceans and reached into infinite space. We are probing the smallest particles of life. . . . But, like the penitent in Kafka's tale 'The Law,' we sit paralyzed before the gates of the human heart."

As always, though, there's a reverse side to the coin. In a fairly recent study made on New York's Lexington Avenue subway, it was found that a great many New Yorkers were anxious and quick to help someone in need. They were, however, selective. For example, they were more apt to help a stricken person if he or she appeared to be a heart-attack victim rather than a drunk (Piliavin et al., 1969).

There are, obviously, no pat answers to the question of why people sometimes help others and sometimes do not. Nevertheless, years of studied concern and concerned studies have produced a number of theories that suggest that terms like "moral callousness," "indifference," "apathy," and "dehumanization" are misleading. The humanitarian impulse is not extinguished by city life; it is merely restrained. The city dweller recognizes that there are practical limitations to altruism in an urban milieu: Were the sensitive individual to give in to every impulse to help those in trouble, he or she would be incapable of leading an even remotely well-ordered life. Although input overload may blunt both the sympathy and the curiosity of an individual, in general the human being does continue to have some sense of social responsibility.

It is the diffusion of this social responsibility, plus social influence, that may largely account for the failure to intervene during emergencies (Darley and Latané, 1968, p. 377). Although each observer knows that others are also watching, it isn't possible to fathom the reactions of the others; the very composure of other witnesses may lead to the conclusion that the event isn't an emergency. Frequently, too, it is assumed that someone has probably already initiated action (by calling the police, for instance). Added to this diffusion of responsibility is the diffusion of any potential blame for inaction. Consequently, Darley and Latané hypothesize, the more bystanders there are, the less likely, or the more slow, any one bystander will be to render aid. In this case, at least, the adage "There's safety in numbers" is shaky.

Consider the dilemma of the bystander:

Faced with a situation in which there is no benefit to be gained for himself, unable to rely on past experience, on the experience of others, or on forethought and planning, denied the opportunity to consider carefully his course of action, the bystander to an emergency is in an unenviable position. It is perhaps surprising that anyone should intervene at all (Latané and Darley, 1969).

There is apt to be little solidarity among bystanders, who after all are usually strangers to one another. In addition, people seem to get mired in a sense of insecurity if they try to cope with an unexpected situation in an unfamiliar setting. To test this notion, an experiment was conducted comparing the response of people in a crowded subway station (a familiar setting) with the response of those in an airport lounge (a less familiar setting). The test subject, posing as a cripple, stumbled and fell near one person, who, being somewhat isolated from others, might alone be expected to help. The score after the incident had been staged in both locales 60 times: twice as many subway riders (83 percent) as airport people (41 percent) helped the man to his feet.

Weighing these results, Latané and Darley speculate that someone who is familiar with his environment and more aware of the way it works "is not overloaded with stimuli. . . . He may have a greater stake in keeping that environment safe. He is in control. Thus he is more likely to help." Cogent as this explanation is, it does not hold true in the case of the Genovese murder, which occurred in a setting highly familiar to the bystanders, their own residential street.

The purported unwillingness of urbanites to help strangers, no matter what the setting, is based in large part on their fear of crime. Considering urban crime statistics, this is hardly an irrational fear. City dwellers feel vulnerable, both physically and emotionally; they barricade themselves in their homes; they sometimes live as though their city were in a state of siege; they become suspicious, wary, and unfriendly in spite of themselves.

Urban friendships, in contrast to rural ones, are not necessarily created and maintained through physical proximity. An urbanite's close friends may be miles away in other parts of the city, while he or she may not know the person next door. All too often, when a crisis hits, the victim is surrounded not by friends but by strangers, and that can apparently make all the difference.

ANONYMITY, LONELINESS, AND ALIENATION

"No more fiendish punishment could be devised, were such a thing physically possible, than that one should be turned loose in society and remain absolutely unnoticed by all the members thereof," wrote William James (1890). There are some who, inclined toward hyperbole, would say that the city has managed to devise such a punishment. Over 26,000 people reside within one square mile of New York City, and over 15,000 in Chicago, in Philadelphia, and in San Francisco. In such a press of humanity—of strangers—individuals become as memorable as lampposts. Certain people retreat gladly into a world of anonymity; others enter that world and despair.

Those who welcome anonymity nurture and guard it. They feel unleashed from stultifying social ties, free to give full rein to their individuality and their eccentricities. In the big city they can, in O. Henry's words, "disappear with the suddenness and completeness of a candle that is blown out." They relish a sense of privacy, the privacy that seems so elusive in rural areas, where "everybody sticks his nose into your business." Paradoxically, some urbanites feel so hemmed in by people that they regard privacy as a blessed state rarely to be attained.

Complete privacy, of course, means either solitude or loneliness. Solitude is a tonic, a reprieve from the needs and demands and sometimes unendurable presence of others, from the socially conditioned assumptions that push a person around, from the masquerades of life. Loneliness, on the other hand, can be painful, unrewarding, and potentially dangerous.

There is the universal, old-fashioned loneliness of a person who is physically alone. But the sense of loneliness that is felt by an urbanite in the midst of a crowd is another story. The urbanite may feel, with Francis Bacon, that "a crowd is not company and faces are but a gallery of pictures and talk but a tinkling cymbal where there is no love." He or she may feel socially isolated or rejected. As Christopher Alexander (1967, p. 60) explains it:

People come to cities for contact. . . . Yet the people who live in cities are often contactless and alienated. A few of them are physically lonely: almost all of them live in a state of endless inner loneliness. They have thousands of contacts, but the contacts are empty and unsatisfying.

The trinity of anonymity, loneliness, and alienation has been the theme of numerous studies, perhaps the most widely read being David Riesman's *The Lonely Crowd* (1952). While both the prevalence and the impact of this trinity in urban milieus are the subject of some dispute (Fischer, 1976), many city planners are gradually coming to the conclusion that there is an impact, that it is considerable, and that it's not good.

Psychologist Phillip Zimbardo (1973) suggests that the anonymity that individuals feel when in the presence of large numbers of people causes them to see others in "de-individuated" ways—as dehumanized categories rather than as unique personalities. So, less inhibited than they would normally be, they are more likely to commit senseless acts of destruction, assaultive aggression, and motiveless murders and to expend an enormous amount of energy shattering traditional institutions, forms, and values.

To test the association between anonymity and aggression, Zimbardo arranged for two cars, seemingly ailing, to be left unattended for 64 hours, one on the street of a small city, Palo Alto, California, near Stanford University, and another on a street across from the Bronx campus of New York University. In both cases the license plates were removed and the hood left open as a come-on for potential vandals. The Palo Alto car was left untouched for over a week (except when, during a rain, a passerby lowered the hood to protect the motor). The Bronx car was, in less than three days, stripped of its usable parts and then smashed almost to pieces. The destructive incidents usually took place in broad daylight and in the presence of passers-by, some of whom stopped to chat with the looters.

Zimbardo's experiment is, of course, open to criticism. The Palo Alto car sat on a quiet, moderately trafficked street leading into the Stanford campus. Many people, passing it day after day, would begin to suspect an experiment and, perversely or not, leave the car unscathed for that very reason. More serious, however, is Claude Fischer's objection (1976): Because the Bronx car, located on a heavily trafficked expressway, was passed by far more people, it was much more exposed to the risk that someone would misbehave. Moreover, says Fischer, the neighborhoods in which the cars were abandoned are of notably different social class, and "the Bronx expressway is a notorious dumping ground for ailing automobiles."

Such criticisms notwithstanding, the association between anonymity and aggression remains. Zimbardo (1973, p. 211) cites many examples of the consequences of induced anonymity, most of them deplorable, but at least one bordering on the absurd. While fixing a flat tire along a highway in Queens, New York, a motorist was startled to see his car's hood being raised and, on investigating, found a stranger taking out the battery. "Take it easy, buddy," said the stranger to his assumed car-stripping colleague, "you can have the tires; all I want is the battery!" Zimbardo comments that "what is being destroyed here is not simply a car, but the basic fabric of social norms which must regulate all communal life." Many times each day in big cities, "young and old, poor and affluent . . . vandalize cars, schools, churches, and almost all symbols of social order." Why this wanton behavior? "If others can't identify or single you out, they can't evaluate, criticize, judge, or punish you; thus, there need be no concern for social evaluation."

Contributing markedly to the anonymity of big-city life is the disintegration or demolition of neighborhoods, those homogeneous "country villages" scattered throughout the city, where people recognize one another and establish networks of conviviality and mutual support. The dissolution of neighborhoods has been recent and massive, stemming largely from well-intentioned efforts to tear down the slums and relocate their inhabitants into more decent surroundings. Yet, however wretched their environment, the slum dwellers at least had a sense of neighborhood. Uprooted and moved into sterile high-rises (which look like fortresses but definitely are not), they now have a sense of anonymity, helplessness, isolation, and fear. As a Chicago architect says of an area in his city (in Terkel, 1967):

> Slum clearance hasn't improved it. They have substituted a more sanitary type of squalor. It is not a shantytown any more, but possibly something worse. It is based on the mistaken premise that you can create a home environment if you give people all the "sanitary" necessities; that you therefore create an atmosphere in which they feel they can live. This is not true. While no one regrets the vanishing of the old slums, we also remember we once had neighborhoods. They have vanished, too. Without them, there can be no such thing as a city to which one feels held.

One of the most significant conclusions to be gleaned out of the piles of studies on forced urban change and its consequences is that the planners' evaluations of a housing area rarely jibe with those of its residents. Planners are concerned mainly with physical design, whereas residents care about both the physical and the social environment. Of course, residents usually adapt to their surroundings (especially if they have no other choice), but that doesn't necessarily mean that they like them. And they will adapt all the more readily if their environment, however inadequate otherwise, gives them a sense of safety (Ittelson et al., 1974).

The corrosive failure of the thoughtless commitment to high-rise housing for the poor, as well as for the more affluent, has led many urban planners to rethink their plans, to consider the intricacies of the human mind as they pore over the intricacies of their blueprints. By relinking monster blocks with the surrounding community (by, for instance, creating new streets in unused space and lining them with row houses, setting up shops and cafes and play areas, and planting trees), some of the ills can be alleviated (Ward, 1976, pp. 118-37). If planning and architecture now and in the future are geared to the social as well as the physical milieu, they may not be a guarantee of delightful neighborhoods. But they will help stem the dangers and discords that are so often the offspring of anonymity and alienation.

NOISE

A city without noise would be eerie, spectral, unnerving. A quiet city, as Max Beerbohm once noted, is a contradiction in terms. The soundscape of a city contributes to its uniqueness. The chiming clocks, church bells, and ship horns all can add to the delight of a city. But when sound becomes annoying or irritating it turns into noise, no matter what its intensity or duration. And of all the urban stressors, noise is probably the most common. The useless din that affects people of all ages, physically and psychologically, night and day, has become so intense that municipalities and citizen groups are finally getting around to fighting it.

Yet back in the Middle Ages, when the cacophony was considerably less, noise abatement was given much more serious attention. Why does the modern urbanite tolerate noise that a 13th-century urbanite wouldn't have dreamed of putting up with? The explanation seems to lie in different modes of perception. The predominant sense today is visual perception; the auditory sense, not used to its full capacity, has therefore become less sensitive. But in the Middle Ages, when artificial light was practically nil and illiteracy nearly universal, the auditory sense was the most keenly developed. The church bell was rung not for esthetic purposes but to convey messages; the town crier served as a "verbal newspaper." Because community survival depended on auditory communication, laws were introduced to reduce noises that were disruptive. (For instance, blacksmiths were prohibited from working in the early morning hours so that their racket wouldn't interfere with anyone's sleep.)

From the Renaissance onward there was a re-ordering of perceptual skills, and gradually the sense of sight overtook the sense of hearing as the chief means of perceiving. Litter, waste, air pollution—these assault our eyes, and we recognize them (although we may not do much about them). But as we can't *see* noise pollution, we tend to tolerate it. So strong is the visual sense that a visual solution is often used to solve a noise problem: If fencing or landscaping is installed around noisy roadways, complaints about noise usually cease although the noise has not been significantly reduced. Such visual screening typifies the current method of problem solving: "If you don't see a problem, there isn't one" (Bragdon, 1970).

Architects design buildings largely for visual impact. Yet, "if only a fraction of the effort applied to the visual aspects of a building were to be expended on acoustical considerations, the world would be a quieter place to live in, and at least one of the major causes of tension could be drastically reduced" (Globe, 1964).

In 1970, noise in many cities was reported to be twice as loud as it was 15 years earlier, and the din continues to mount. If projections for the increase in population, the size of cities, and noise levels hold true, "the world of 2025 might well be populated by a race of half-deaf neurotics" (Still, 1970). The noise level is already so high in major U.S. cities that at least half the inhabitants are expected to suffer gradual or partial deafness.

Until recently it was not realized that noise levels encountered in cities frequently exceed the standards found to be injurious in industry. Urban society takes in more and more devices with higher and higher noise outputs; and an increasing number of people use those devices. Motor vehicles, construction equipment, air conditioners, household appliances, garbage disposals, electric toothbrushes—all contribute their share to the din to which, unfortunately, people have become habituated. Urbanites seldom attribute the changes in their moods or behavior to the noises that assault them.

Tolerance of noise is largely subjective: "One man's music may be another man's noise" (Bragdon, 1970), as anyone who dislikes acid rock can acidly attest. Neurotics apparently suffer more from noise than do "normals." To someone with a hangover the tinkle of a spoon against a teacup can sound like a machine-gun barrage. (W.C. Fields once complained, when hung over as usual, about the racket of the Alka-Seltzer fizzing in the glass.) Other people's children often seem noisier than one's own. But this variation in human response decreases the louder the noise gets.

The bothersomeness of urban blare appears to follow life rhythms. That is, a noise may be more irritating at night than during the day, and on weekends than on weekdays. Annoyance induced by noise creates a feeling of resentment that one's physical privacy, or one's thoughts, have been invaded. Most annoying (Berland, 1970) are the sounds that are:

Loud—the louder the noise, the more annoying it is.

High-pitched . . .

Intermittent and irregular—the more randomly the noise occurs, the more annoying it is.

Produced from a hidden or moving source—the more uncertain you are about where noise is coming from, the more annoying it is.

Inappropriate to your own activities—we seldom object to the noise *we* make.

Unexpected—like sonic booms, noise can startle.

Unwanted sound, whether the source is Muzak or a drill, is pervasive and penetrating. Auditory privacy is far less easy to achieve than visual privacy because the sense of hearing works around the clock. The urbanite is constantly vulnerable to noise, and its effects on physical and psychological health are incalculable. The noise that is consciously perceived may be regarded as a nuisance (as the city is a place where a cry for help or a cry of pain may be ignored as just another city sound), but it can interfere with thought processes, disrupt communication, impair performance, disturb sleep, and foment general mental stress. It is all too easy to underestimate the harmful consequences of noise: Once it has stopped, irritation declines, but the endocrine system continues to react for some time (Saarinen, 1976).

The insidious nature of noise, which has a more profound physiological impact than the conscious perception of noise, is not usually recognized. For adaptation to noise is made at the intellectual, not the physiological, level. It is possible to lose up to 40 percent of hearing before the permanent impairment is even noticed. Those who listen to high-intensity rock music for a total of more than 23 hours within a two-month period may suffer irreversible hearing loss. Twenty minutes on a subway can affect hearing for about 40 minutes afterwards; and 25 to 30 years of daily subway rides can cause permanent damage. In addition to hearing loss, it is believed that noise contributes to the onset of certain stress-related diseases such as hypertension, peptic ulcer, and colitis; that it exacerbates or perpetuates a disease after it has developed; and that it may accelerate the aging processes. (Some of the physiological effects of noise are a bit odd: A group of people subjected to a loud noise for 15 minutes were found to be color-blind for over an hour afterwards.)

Noise can be particularly harmful when someone is already under stress for it leads, understandably, to an intense feeling of helplessness to combat it. According to a recent study, people living within three miles of Los Angeles Airport suffered a 29 percent higher rate of nervous disorders than did those living six miles away, whereas another study in England revealed a 31 percent increase in nervous disorders among persons living close to London's Heathrow Airport. (McLean and Tarnopolsky, 1977). When undue noise is inflicted upon shaky personalities, it can apparently, on occasion, push them over the brink. For example, in New York City a man who shot and killed a boy who was playing noisily outside his window explained to the police that he was a night worker and all the ruckus was disturbing his daytime sleep.

Not surprisingly, traffic noise is the biggest offender in the urban cacophony because of its prevalence and loudness. Yet people seem to condone this noise more than others simply because they depend on motor vehicles for so much of their transportation. The debilitating effects of heavy traffic, however, can be long-term and subtle. For example, grammar-school children living in an apartment-house complex adjacent to an expressway were found to have impaired reading ability. Those on the higher, quieter floors of 32-story buildings had higher scores; those on the lower floors, where noise was more obtrusive, had lower scores. The longer the children lived in these buildings, the more impaired their reading ability became.

Still another strike against urban noise is its apparent effect on social relations. This was borne out in a study of three residential streets of San Francisco, one with light traffic, the second with moderate traffic, and the third with heavy traffic. Residents on the heavy-traffic street complained that the noise was "too much," felt they were living in a restricted environment, had little pride in the appearance of their street, and enjoyed little social interaction. By contrast, the street with light traffic was relatively quiet and encouraged the residents to form a friendly, close-knit community that cared how its lively street looked. Paradoxically, on the moderately trafficked street, residents turned out to be more dissatisfied than the inhabitants subjected to heavy traffic. Why? Although they didn't experience pronounced discomfort, they expected more of their environment, and in their disappointment failed to nurture a genuine sense of community on this in-between street. Naturally, the extent of traffic hazards and congestion had some bearing, too, on the attitudes and perceptions of the residents of each street (Appleyard & Lintell, 1972).

The quietest city in the United States is believed to be Memphis, a community that several years ago mobilized for action against noise and proved that the problem is not insoluble. The noisiest city in the world is reportedly Tokyo. Although Tokyo has some of the most advanced and imaginative noise-control laws of any city in the world, they are hard to implement: Houses made of wood and with thin exterior walls lean against one another; many small factories and cottage industries are located right in the middle of housing (Kavaler, 1974).

Urbanites around the world are making a noise about noise, with the result that noise-control laws are proliferating (although they are, alas, far easier to put on the books than to put into practice). David Lipscomb (1974), an international authority on noise control, predicted in 1974 that "an astounding number of noise abatement and control breakthroughs probably will occur in the next decade." In the meantime, the best immediate remedy is a pair of earplugs.

In the sixteenth century the redoubtable Leonardo da Vinci, affronted by the congestion, disorder, and squalor of the city of Milan, suggested to the Duke of Milan that ten cities be designed, each limited to about 30,000 inhabitants. Had his advice been taken, it might have started a commendable trend.

Of course, no setting or situation is ideal all the time or for everyone. Utopia is a nonplace; it does not and probably cannot exist except, perhaps, as a state of mind. It is an ideal to strive for (Sommer, 1969). But most cities today are not even remotely striving for Utopia; and many of their inhabitants are merely trying to cope with the stress and realities of urban life, leaving idealism far behind.

All too often planners and architects ignore or are ignorant of human nature. The stress of urban life is frequently a direct result of the insensitivity of designers to the cultural backgrounds, the needs, and the hopes of the users of a built environment. The anonymous Chicago architect quoted earlier (Terkel, 1967) pleads for architecture that is something other than "a piece of advertising." Commenting philosophically on the tangled web of complexities modern urban life has woven, he says:

> We're caught in a treadmill we created. . . . If we, as St. Francis of Assisi, were of that simplicity of spirit, it might change. But that is not the way of the world, see?

> And yet, in the individual must lie the way out, because he is society. It can't be ordered. It must be achieved. The achievement is so simple. It probably will not be done. Everybody looks for miracles, wonders. . . . You long for something not wonderful, for something that is simple, yet is *yours.* You get tired of wonders. In the simplehearted person, finally, is the solution. A society so pervaded will make it. Not the doctrine of the announced idea.

A decade has passed since these words were written. We're still waiting for solutions and for more simplehearted persons.

Lines or Queues:
Where Do They Lead?

Chapter 6

There was already a long line at the theater. So we had our usual discussions: Should we bother? Even after waiting an hour would we get in? Jan insisted we wait since we'd already taken the time to get ready and drive to the theater. So we did. I passed at least 200 people on the way to the ticket office while Jan raced to the end of the line to establish our spot.

While we stood there among innumerable wary strangers, all my territorial instincts flared up, my glands releasing adrenalin, preparing me for combat or flight or for some unknown. With every new group of people to arrive my chest constricted, and secretly I'd follow them with my eyes, suspecting that each person was somehow calculating how to sneak into line further up. At the same time I occasionally made flapping motions to make sure that the people right around us didn't edge into any small space between us and the people in front. By the time the line started moving, I was extremely tense, well on my way to the headache that solidified during the film.

This scenario is not from the files of a paranoid schizophrenic. It recounts universal feelings identifiable by most people. What civilized, or even uncivilized, adult has not felt the tedium, the frustration, the slow-burning anger, the stress of standing and waiting in line?

Queues are the by-products of life in any densely populated area where people must compete for goods and services.

> Outside Havana's ice cream parlors . . . Cubans stand in line for two hours for a dish of six-flavor ice cream while in Mexico City, commuters wait patiently in line to catch a . . . shared, fixed-route taxicab. In Tokyo, people wait in lines outside real estate development offices for as long as two weeks hoping to buy a block of land for a home site. Queues of shoppers form at dawn in Rangoon, Burma, to buy rice, bread, and soap. . . . And somewhere in Nigeria, long lines of Biafrans wait patiently for a turn to wash their clothes at a primitive outdoor laundry (Helmer and Eddington, 1973).

Queues are everywhere: supermarkets, restaurants, department stores, libraries, theaters, post offices, toll booths, banks, public transport, and playgrounds. Queues have become so integrated into modern urban society that they have evolved into a culture of their own with rules and traditions. At the height of the Australian football season, for example, thousands of fans queue up overnight outside Melbourne Stadium in order to be assured of a ticket. Such a wait represents a sizeable investment of time and energy. To cut down on this waste a person joins the queue as part of a small group and takes his turn in spending one hour on to every three hours off. A person who queues alone and needs to leave for brief periods can "stake a claim" by leaving some item of personal property such as a labeled box, folding chair, or sleeping bag. But if he fails to show up within two or three hours the claim might be tossed aside or even burned.

Overnight queues for tickets to the Metropolitan Opera House in New York are highly organized, regulated by the first person in line. This person, known as the "keeper of the list," registers each member of the queue in order of arrival and holds a roll call every couple of hours. Except for mandatory reporting at the roll calls the members of the queue are free to wander as they please. These roll calls used to occur regularly throughout the night until New

York's crime rate scared the queuers off. Now the Metropolitan queue disbands in the evening and reconvenes around 7:00 a.m. (Helmer and Eddington, 1973).

Queues are governed by several definite social principles. The overriding principle is first come, first served. That's fine if you're first. But the hard correlate of that principle is that one waits one's turn. Waiting one's turn fulfills the minimal conditions of the Golden Rule, i.e., you don't jump into the line ahead of anyone else because you know if you do, he will probably do the same to you.

Queues are sometimes regulated by the server. Based on the social principle of first come, first served, the server ordinarily tries to coordinate his order of service with appointments or the order of arrival. To make it easier to keep track of the order, the server sometimes tries to facilitate queuing by providing ecological supports, such as channels with painted lines, cords, rails, and even with outlines of human feet walking exactly where you are to go. Better, you may find the mechanical number dispenser or the restaurant waiting list. With those options, the "waiter" can avoid standing in line. However, most places have chaotic queuing systems or, as in subways and at sales counters, no system at all.

Of course, there are several other principles that allow exceptions to the first come, first served rule. In some instances services are granted first to those who need them most, however long it takes to administer. Most obviously, victims in emergency rooms of the hospital must be treated on the latter basis. Another group often authorized as exceptions are those with minimal service needs. Shoppers with few items and cash are granted the express lane, and post offices and banks allow a special queue for those with needs that can be quickly taken care of. Within each preemptive category, however, the rule of first come, first served prevails.

The very persistence of the queuing rule is proof of the general inclination toward what it prohibits. The rails, cords, and number dispensers evidence the fact that waiting while a service is being rendered another person runs contrary to human nature. Observe any mother trying to socialize a two-year-old who wants to play on the slide with other children. The lesson taught is wait your turn, but it's not an easy one. And in fact, some people never learn it.

Consequently, there are several deterrents to jumping the queue. One is the fear of being torn apart by other queuers. Or if not that, at least a fear of the scene that would ensue and possibly some humiliating embarrassment. The worst that could happen—given that the queue jumper survives—is that he might not get waited on at all if the server understands that he has jumped the line: The server knows that to tolerate such behavior would not be good for his business, and he probably identifies with the people waiting in line. For these reasons, attempts to jump the queue are usually made surreptitiously.

Some queuing situations lend themselves to various by-passes. For example, people are fast to fill in gaps in cafeteria lines where others are slow to choose. In the market express line shoppers often try to get by with more items than allowed and easily pretend innocence when caught. Sometimes it's possible to jump lines by having friends save a place or by finding a proxy, e.g., in the betting lines. Another legal means of beating the queue is to save your place in the market line with a shopping cart while you gather the last few things. For the most part though, no one likes to think he's waiting his turn while someone else is sneaking special attention.

PSYCHOLOGICAL DIMENSIONS OF WAITING

What is it about waiting, particularly waiting in a line with other people, that is so annoying? Is it that you must give up a better use of your time? Is it that you must submit to someone else's master plan and let someone else control your own time, whether or not you would be actually doing something more productive? Is it the boredom of waiting? Is it anxiety that whatever service you are after—tickets to a theater, getting in to see the doctor—will have run out by the time you get there?

To wait is after all to remain in a state of expectation. It is the experience of the *incomplete gestalt,* a state of imbalance and even

dissonance. Waiting is one form of doing nothing. It imposes con-
straints on attention, drawing attention to time itself, which passes
all the more slowly because it is attended to. Bettelheim (1965) has
said that waiting is "likely to be experienced as empty but nevertheless exhausting, and above all as boring. This feeling of unpleasantness or boredom is the overt expression of unconscious
anxiety, or at least of strong tensions without any definite or
conscious content." Waiting is costly in terms of human wear and
tear.

One problem with waiting is that suddenly one is set loose with
nothing to do but probe his own head and feelings. It appears that
the socially disengaged self is freed only to become its own burden.
Unfortunately, the waiter cannot become completely involved
even in self—through reverie or sleep—because he might miss his
turn or delay others. Rather he must remain alert to the situation,
looking for signals of his impending turn. Because he must keep
one ear or eye on his goal, time is something to be killed because it
cannot be utilized. There is no fully efficient way to cope with the
distress of waiting.

The primary distress of waiting is that it limits the productive
use of time and thereby *generates* distinct personal and social costs.
Not only is the waiter in a state of unfulfillment, he also lacks control over desired or necessary resources. Liberman (1968), a Russian economist, observes that waiting involves enormous costs in
unproductivity. For him the problem of delay in waiting rooms
and queues merits the status of a social problem.

Another psychological dimension to the distress of waiting is the
effect of subordination. One who is in position to cause another to
wait has power over him. To be kept waiting implies that one's
own time is less valuable than that of the one who imposes the wait.
The apology ensuing the wait period, "Sorry to keep you waiting,"
confirms this: The main feature of the apology is that the tardiness
was unintentional and therefore not to be taken personally as an
evaluation of the worth of the victim's time.

The powerful, however, are immune to such norms: with doc-
tors and judges, the unequal apportionment of worthiness is taken

for granted by superordinates. A sense of degradation inheres in waiting when delay implies that the client is the less worthy party in such a relationship. The suppliant inferior is unable to satisfy needs other than through the actions of a superior whose dominance hinges on his being uniquely able to provide for them.

The discomforts of waiting may be compounded when one waits with others. Queues of more than one person mean social involvement, monitoring others, and some types of interaction. One is subjected to the presence of non-acquaintances in whose presence one may feel uneasy. This is especially true in cases of super-subordinate relationships such as might occur in an executive elevator. Again there is the sense of being intruded upon if one must wait in the company of people one considers contaminated or inferior, e.g., carriers of diseases in hospitals, a person with a cold on a bus, people with strong odors or dirty clothes or bodies, and other historically contaminated people.

The form of the queue lends itself to a feeling of contamination because of the face-to-back structure. Schwartz (1975) suggests that symbolically the back portion of one's body has long been a source of subordination and debasement in western society. It has always been rude to turn one's back on another. In addition, the backside is the portion of the body most difficult to groom and for this reason is most likely to be unknowingly rumpled, stained, or sweaty. Not only might it be unpleasant to have to face someone else's back, the queuer is also compelled to expose his own without an opportunity to guarantee its fitness for presentation. People often feel "watched" and fear they may not be presenting the self they intend to. Many people experience the common paranoid feelings that possibly people are disapproving of them. "Get off my back. Don't breathe down my neck." Queuing puts us in the ambiguous situation of not knowing what impression we make on those behind us. In most lines interqueuer distance is greater at the tail end than in the middle, and persons tend to position themselves perpendicularly to the line so that they can avoid visual contamination by persons in front "while simultaneously exercising peripheral surveillance on the monitoring activity of the person in back" (Schwartz,

1975). Queue members, in fact, appear to be totally unmindful of one another, as if denying the disturbing proximity of those nearby.

ALTERNATIVE ATTITUDES TOWARD QUEUING

To cope with the frustration of standing relatively idle in a less than comfortable environment, most people spend a lot of time rationalizing the benefits of the reward at the end of the queue. Some even attempt to turn the wait period into a positive pleasure. Melbourne football fans erect tents, stretch out on cots, build campfires, and consume quantities of liquor while waiting in line. Thus, a mammoth queue is rationalized as a social occasion. Some people claim it to be the social event of the year. One avid fan said: "People are always knocking queues. What I would like to know is what people like myself would do without them?"

The same "justifying" attitude toward time spent in queuing is found in a survey of ticket lines for the Rolling Stones concert at Boston Garden.

There were approximately 600 college students communing together on blankets and sleeping bags. The sweet smell of marijuana hung in the air. During the night, many of the kids had met up with old friends or made new ones. To one of our questions, "How do you feel about having to wait in line?" a Radcliffe girl answered, "I'm really excited. It's kind of a social event." A Boston University student told us, "It's a groovy way to meet people" (Helmer and Eddington, 1973).

In Russia, as consumer goods are scarce; shoppers must stand in lines to obtain both luxuries and necessities. These lines also tend to be more complicated. To make a single purchase, it is common for a shopper to have to stand in one line to order an item, run to another line to pay for it, and run to a third to pick it up—provided, of course, that it hasn't disappeared from the shelves (Smith, 1976).

But in the USSR such lines appear to have become an accepted way of life, and oddly enough they have been rationalized as a source of satisfaction. Russian shoppers pride themselves in their ability to form lines and shift from one line to another for several hours each day. They develop skills at estimating just how fast a queue is moving so that they can have their places saved and thus stand in several lines simultaneously. One Russian journalist writes:

> In America if your wife has bought a nice new dress and I notice it, I will say, "Oh yes, that's nice," and that's all. But in Moscow, when I get my hands on a pair of shoes that I like, it is an achievement, a feat, an exploit. It means that I have managed to work it out in some complicated way through a friend or perhaps I have found a sales clerk to bribe or I have gone from store to store and I have stood in line for hours. Notice how I put it, not simply "bought some shoes" but "got my hands on a pair of shoes." So when I get the shoes I like, I am very proud of them . . . (Smith, 1976).

In England and Germany queues are a source of national pride (Hall, 1969). In those countries queues are considered as a living testament to the value of voluntarily structured civilization. Even in the U.S. we perceive the queue as a democratic process and enjoy the notion that rank and possessions don't count there.

To some businessmen, the queue is a great commercial boon. Imagine how impractical and costly it would be to employ enough bank tellers to avoid the formation of lines in any crowded bank. Or imagine a theater with a ticket taker for every person standing in line. Of course, theater owners long ago discovered that long queues are good advertising. And it is true that queuing weeds out those who don't really care enough to stand in line. Popular plays, operas, movies, concerts, sports events, and the like are therefore guaranteed—by virtue of the lines that precede them—a dedicated and attentive audience.

Fortunately, a few technological advances have shortened the amount of time that people are obliged to stand in line. During New York's World Fair of 1964, the crush of people waiting to see Michelangelo's "Pieta" was so great that Fair officials arranged for visitors to view the sculpture from three tiers of slowly moving conveyor belts. Ordering tickets by computer for theatrical events and transportation is now common, and computers in banks and stores cut out some of the credit-checking time. Even so, there are still rather long lines in front of the computerized ticket outlets and at banks and department stores. And the joy of being hauled past Michelangelo's "Pieta" on a conveyor belt is surely mingled with other feelings and sensations.

No matter how efficient the line or how advanced the technology, lines still exist. They are symptomatic of our crowded world. In a sense, we are spawning ourselves into a continuous huge, noisy, traffic jam. And the frustrations and aggravations that come from the delays we meet in dealing with long lines of humanity promote aggression. It almost seems that the queue exists to remind us of more basic animal instincts, for even among the most passive, the queue can bring out fiercely aggressive behavior.

Crowding and Aggression

Chapter 7

Some of the best-known studies of animal crowding are those of the research psychologist John Calhoun (1962) who used rats and mice as his experimental subjects. In his first study, Calhoun placed five pregnant, wild Norway rats in a quarter-acre (10,000 square feet) outdoor enclosure, provided them with ample food, water, and freedom from predators, and then sat back to watch their behavior and population dynamics over a period of 28 months.

What happened was somewhat surprising. In theory, it would have been biologically possible for the rat population to increase from 5 to 5,000 in the 28 months. It was also theoretically possible for the rats to remain alive and healthy in the quarter-acre pen, just as 5,000 rats have done when confined to small cages inside a 10,000 square-foot area. In reality, however, the number of wild rats grew to a mere 200 and then stabilized at 150. What caused this seeming self-control on the part of the rats? Calhoun accounts for it by stating that 5,000 rats simply cannot exist together in a single 10,000 square-foot area.

Not only was 5,000 too many rats for Calhoun's pen, but even 150 of the animals had trouble coexisting in the area. With free run of the pen and equally free choice of companions, the rats organized themselves into 13 local colonies of approximately 12 individuals, which seems to be the maximum number of rats that can live together with any degree of harmony. Even in groups of this size, fighting became so disruptive of normal rat-rearing practices that only a few infants were able to survive, thus stabilizing their numbers at 150.

Calhoun's second study, which expands the conclusions of the first, produced even more dramatic results. In this study, Calhoun placed 32 adult rats of both sexes in a 10 by 14 foot room divided into four pens connected by ramps that allowed all the rats access to all of the pens. Each pen was a complete dwelling unit, with food hopper, drinking trough, places to nest, and nesting materials—a satisfactory setting for the development of communities similar to those observed in the semi-wild conditions of the first experiment. Had the rats followed that pattern, they might have been expected to form four initial colonies of about eight individuals, with population stabilizing at about 48 under conditions of fighting and stress.

What happened, instead, was that the rat population burgeoned to 80 adults within 12 months. After this, Calhoun began removing surplus infants in order to keep the population at 80. The aim of this ratnapping was to maintain three generations of rats at a population density just double that which had produced definitely observable stress in the "wild." (Calhoun reasoned that if the rats were allowed to increase to greater numbers it would be just a matter of time until the stress of overcrowding would impair their reproductive functions to the point that the colonies would die out.)

THE BEHAVIORAL SINK

The result of this "double stress" situation was a phenomenon Calhoun called a *behavioral sink* or, "the outcome of any behavioral process that collects animals together in unusually great

numbers. The unhealthy connotations of the term are not acci-
dental: a behavioral sink does act to aggravate all forms of pathology
that can be found within a group" (p. 144).

In the events leading up to the development of the sink, two
dominant male rats staked out territories in the two end pens,
where each maintained a harem of eight to ten females and produced colonies similar to the natural groupings seen in the wild.
The rest of the rats (approximately 60 in number) were forced into
the two middle pens, where they lived, ate, reproduced, and reared
their young under conditions of extreme crowding. In this situation, the rats became conditioned to eating only in the company of
other rats, voluntarily choosing to eat at the crowded food hoppers
in the two center pens, while the hoppers in the end pens were used
only rarely. The satisfactions of this behavior were evidently more
social than gastronomic.

The sink itself was manifested by a total disruption of most of
the rats' former habits. These disruptions occurred in social organization, sexual behavior, nest building, and other activities. The
stressful consequences were particularly visible among females,
who rarely succeeded in bringing their pregnancies to term. When
they did, they frequently did not survive the delivery of their litters.

Among the other behaviors reported by Calhoun were hyper-
activity, increased aggressiveness among males, sexual deviation,
cannibalism, and withdrawal from other animals:

> An estrous female would be pursued relentlessly by a pack of males,
> unable to escape their soon unwanted attentions. . . . Nearly half of
> the first-and second-generation females that lived in the behavioral-
> sink situation had died of these causes by the end of the 16th month.
> . . . At regular intervals during the course of their waking hours, the
> top-ranking males engaged in free-for-alls that culminated in the trans-
> fer of dominance from one male to another. . . . The most normal
> males exhibited occasional signs of pathology, going berserk, attacking
> females, juveniles and the less active males, and showing a particular
> predilection—which rats do not normally display—for biting other
> animals on the tail. . . . As soon as a female returned to a burrow, a
> prober would follow her inside. On these expeditions the probers often

found dead young lying in the nests; as a result they tended to become cannibalistic in the later months of a population's history.

If rats were the only creatures seriously disrupted by crowding, Calhoun's sink might be dismissed as an interesting, if slightly gruesome, anomaly. But there is evidence that many other animals grow disturbed in conditions of extreme population density.

In a study of rhesus monkeys, for instance, one experimenter (Southwick, 1967) discovered that aggression among a troop of animals increased sharply when their outdoor cage was decreased to half its original size.

Two other researchers (Alexander and Roth, 1971) tried an extreme short-term version of the experiment on a group of monkeys they had captured as an intact troop. After leaving the monkeys undisturbed for two-and-a-half years in a two-acre enclosure where they lived as an integrated, stable social group, the experimenters put them into a pen only 2.3 percent as large as their previous area. During the four days of their acute crowding, the monkeys displayed an increase in both mild and severe aggression against each other.

This increased aggression was seen in both males and females in the troop. Males, however, inflicted and suffered more attacks than did females, who seemed the least affected by the crowding. Low-ranking adult males and juveniles were the most frequent victims of attacks, while adult females suffered the fewest.

When the monkeys were returned to their two-acre enclosure, the severe forms of aggression disappeared, and the milder forms diminished to baseline levels. The researchers hypothesized that "the effect of severe aggression was due to removal from a familiar habitat, rather than increased density, and that crowding per se produced the increase in mild aggression" (p. 88).

So far, of course, we have discussed only the artificially produced crowding of animals. Is there any evidence that similar disruptions of behavior occur among animals in their natural environments? Several field studies suggest that some of what happens in pens also happens in nature when animals feel crowded, and that an inborn territoriality is a major factor in producing the feeling of crowdedness.

In his book *The Territorial Imperative,* Robert Ardrey (1966) reports on a number of field observations of animal territoriality and aggression. One of these is the observation by Dale Jenkins of a family of terrible-tempered blue geese as they successfully defended their territory against a series of invaders. Somehow, Jenkins managed to keep count of the number of pecks delivered in each battle and recorded the following statistics: Blue geese vs. Canada geese: Blue, 259, Canada, 0. Blue geese vs. mallard ducks: Blue, 44, Mallard, 0. Blue geese vs. snow geese: Blue, 185, Snow, 13.

With pecking scores like these for the home team, it is clear that blue geese, at least, are able to muster an impressive amount of aggressive energy whenever they sense a threat to their territory. There is evidence that such behavior is common in the animal world, though it is manifested differently from one species to the next.

In a study of roe deer in the forests of southern England, Richard Prior (cited by Ardrey, p. 78) discovered that a roe buck will protect a particular doe (not necessarily his previous year's mate) and her fawns in a particular territory where they are insured privacy and an exclusive food supply. When two watchful roe bucks meet at a mutual boundary, they exchange a series of aggressive threats. But instead of going on to fight each other, the bucks vent their rage on the forest. With iron-hard bare antlers, "they will attack all convenient trees with a racket to be heard hundreds of yards."

From such observations, Prior concluded that "if too many roe bucks share the forest, then each will have a territory too small for its energy, rage at the border will be at a maximum, and fraying and damage to trees at its most disastrous" (p. 80).

Such activity is called *displacement activity,* which Ardrey defines as follows: "When we are confronted by two opposite courses of action—to fight or to flee, for example, or to prolong our insults or apologize—we tend for the moment to take a predictable third course of action unrelated to the other two" (p. 87).

Such displacement activity is, of course, not limited to England's roe deer population. Mutual antagonism between herring gulls produces a territorial flap in which the birds beat their wings, make violent threats at each other, and climax the performance by furiously pulling up grass.

Male sticklebacks, a highly territorial fish, settle their property disputes by chasing each other back and forth across invisible boundary lines and then standing on their heads to dig holes in the sand, all the while staring at each other with goggle-eyed loathing.

HUMAN BEHAVIOR

These and other examples of animal reactions to crowding—or even the threat of it—would make it appear than many animals are genetically programmed for instinctive acts of aggression, both direct and "displaced," in defense of their home territories. Are human animals included in this programming? A growing body of evidence suggests that they may be. If we begin with military history, for example, we will find it replete with accounts of small bands of soldiers who have managed to defend their territories against seemingly insurmountable odds.

What accounts for such incredible feats? One explanation is that inflamed patriotic passions in humans are similar to aroused territorial instincts in animals and that both serve to unleash vast amounts of aggressive energy. But war, it can certainly be argued, is not "everyday life." To see a link between crowding and everyday human aggression, we need to see examples somewhat closer to "home."

A casual glance at any big-city newspaper adds support to what many researchers claim: that crime rates are high in the populous inner-cities and ghettos and lower in the less-crowded suburbs. This pattern seems to hold true even in the supposed paradise of Hawaii. In a study of adult and juvenile crime in Honolulu, one researcher (Schmitt, 1957) found that areas with large households tended to produce more juvenile offenders than did low-density neighborhoods and concluded that high densities predispose resident populations, both juvenile and adult, to illegal activity.

It should be noted that Schmitt's findings indicate only two measures to be related to juvenile and adult crime rates: population per acre and dwellings with more than 1.51 persons per room.

Other researchers have gone beyond "crime rates" in attempting to refine measures of density and crowding as they relate to aggression. One French study reported that people reached a threshold of psychological crowding when between 2 and 2.5 individuals occupied a room. When this threshold was exceeded, the investigators found a direct relationship between crowding and aggression as well as other antisocial behavior (Chombart de Lauwe, 1959, cited in Zlutnik and Altman, 1972, p. 48).

Another study (Galle et al., 1972) used census tract data in an attempt to correlate population density with a range of pathological behaviors in 75 community areas of Chicago. Their measure of asocial, aggressive behavior was the "number of male individuals brought before the Family Court of Cook County on delinquency petitions during the years 1958-61 per 100 male population 12-16 years of age in 1960." Their measures of density were: persons per room, rooms per housing unit, housing units per structure, and residential structures per acre.

Galle and his associates found that although each of these factors had some impact on pathological behavior, the strongest relationships were with "interpersonal press," which the authors define as the number of persons per room and number of rooms per housing unit. According to Galle et al., the component of "interpersonal press" that most affects juvenile delinquency is the number of persons per room, "where the escalation of both social demands and the need to inhibit desires would become particularly problematic."

Crowding tends to cause a marked increase in bothersome stimuli, and it may conflict with a basic instinct if humans—as many other animals—have a biological need for territory or privacy. Galle speculates that:

> People . . . react to the incessant demands, stimulation, and lack of privacy resulting from overcrowding with irritability, weariness and withdrawal. Furthermore, people are likely to be so . . . involved in

reacting to their environment that it becomes extremely difficult for them to step back, look at themselves, and plan ahead [or] follow through on their plans. Thus, we might expect the behavior of human beings in an overcrowded environment to be primarily a response to their immediate situation and to reflect relatively little regard for the long-range consequences of their acts.

Galle states that juvenile delinquents from crowded homes are found to possess a high degree of *autonomy,* including a decrease in the desire to communicate with others. It seems likely that crowding can foster this attitude. With no privacy, no place to do homework without noise and interruption, experiencing friction with irritable, often unhappy parents, children seek relief from their "high density" homes and go elsewhere to vent their frustrations.

Crowded parents, too, seem to desire some autonomy from their children and are likely to welcome their absence, at least temporarily. The resulting situation does not permit parents to supervise or even keep in touch with their children's outside activities, and the lack of parental supervision may make children more susceptible to peer influence and the lure of illegal activity.

Such speculations, of course, are incomplete when based only on census tract and epidemiological data, as are Galle's findings. Other factors such as socioeconomic status and cultural attitudes are undoubtedly linked to the incidence of social pathology.

Cultural differences in people's reactions to crowding can be seen in a comparison of surveys from different parts of the world. For example, according to Chombart de Lauwe, rates of social disorganization begin to rise in the homes of French workers when there are less than 8-10 square meters of space per person, per dwelling.

In Hong Kong, however, Schmitt found that people living at a density level of 13 persons per acre with average household space of 32 square feet per person (less than half the lower space limit required by the French workers) still maintained low rates of adult and juvenile delinquency.

To further confuse the issue, two Dutch researchers (Levy and Herzog, 1974) recorded a *negative* correlation between crowding and aggressive crimes (i.e., murder and assault). Their explanation is that in Holland, "the family is a bastion, a retreat, a sanctuary," and thus "a large family [more persons per dwelling] is a source of more protection against stress and the source of more varied and interesting experiences and interactions." Also, according to Levy and Herzog, "aggressive impulses are carefully regulated in Dutch society, and physical violence is highly uncommon."

Nonetheless, these last examples do not rule out a relationship between population pressures and social pathology. In Holland, for instance, the connection between area density and *property* offenses seems very strong. The point to consider is that human space requirements and attitudes toward crowding can vary significantly from culture to culture.

It appears, then, that crowding or density per se is neither a positive nor a negative factor in human behavior. Just as oxygen alone does not make fire, other factors besides high density must be present for the "combustion" of aggressive behavior. As suggested earlier, socioeconomic factors probably contribute to crime rates.

A heretofore "innocent bystander," the urban landscape, may also be involved in the genesis of crime. One study (Newman, 1973) suggests that crime rates increase in close linear approximation to building heights. The effects of building height, argues Newman, are somewhat independent of both population density and the number of units per housing project (although, beyond limits, increased density leads almost inevitably to increased building height). Newman believes that certain types of low-rise architectural design give residents the feeling of protective ownership and heighten their awareness of the territorial boundaries between occupants. Thus, a suitably low-profile architectural scheme could conceivably produce lower crime rates even in high-density areas.

Weather, too, has been seen to affect crime rates in overcrowded areas. Heat in particular, when combined with crowded conditions, is thought to contribute to aggressive behavior, from isolated incidents of arguing, "needling," and fist-fighting through full-scale mass rioting. In a report on the 1968 ghetto riots, the United States Riot Commission noted that 9 out of 10 disorders occurred on days when the temperature was 90 degrees Fahrenheit or higher. (Temperature, of course, was not the only factor. The Commission also cited crowded ghetto living conditions as a probable cause of the rioting.)

Observations such as these inspired Griffitt and Veitch (1971) to look a little more closely at the effects of "effective temperature and population density on social-affective behavior in humans." In other words, these researchers guessed that people would feel less friendly toward each other on hot days than they would on cool days. They also hypothesized that people would regard each other more negatively under conditions of crowding. Their experiment confirmed their hypothesis: Subjects liked each other less at 93.5 degrees Fahrenheit than they did at 73.4 degrees. They also liked each other less when many people were crowded into one room.

An interesting sidelight of the study is that the subjects imagined themselves to be warmer in a crowded room than in an uncrowded room, even though temperatures in both were identical. This, according to Griffitt and Veitch, suggests that "hot weather" (or negative) interpersonal responses may occur in crowded conditions where only moderate temperatures prevail.

Only a few other studies have examined the relationship of population density to aggression. In one of these, Hutt and Vaizey (1966) observed groups of autistic, brain-damaged, and normal children engaged in "free play" in a room about 480 square feet in area. Their assumption was that, as group size was increased from a minimum of 6 to a maximum of 12, the autistic children would react, in an exaggerated way, as would "introverted or relatively inhibited" normal individuals, and that the brain-damaged children would show, in exaggerated form, the reactions of "extroverted" individuals in the normal population. The behaviors to be measured were aggression (fighting, snatching, and toy breaking), social interaction, and the amount of time spent by children on the outer boundaries of the room.

The results of the study showed that brain-damaged children became more aggressive with each increase in group size, while normal children became significantly more aggressive only when the group reached its maximum size of 12. The autistic children showed a negligible amount of aggression in any sized group.

In terms of their social interactions, the brain-damaged children showed more interaction in the medium-sized groups (7-11 children), autistics showed less interaction in the large groups, and normals showed more autonomy and less social interaction in the larger groups.

In a later experiment, Hutt and McGrew (1967) examined the effects of social density by changing the size of the area rather than the size of the group (all of whom were "normals" in this case). They found that a group of nursery school children became more aggressive with adults and with one another as social density increased in smaller play areas.

In another study (reviewed by Freedman, 1972) McGrew tried altering both the size of the group and the size of the area, observing children at play in two rooms, one of them 593 square feet in area, the other 778 square feet. In both rooms, there was more aggressive behavior when 16 children were present than when 8 children played in the room.

Everything we have seen so far points up the fact that the relationship between crowding and aggression is exceedingly complex. There seems to be no way to examine these phenomena without also considering factors like instincts, territoriality, culture, socioeconomics, weather, individual predispositions (i.e., brain damage, autism), building height, the social environment, and finally and inevitably sex.

Sex, as several studies have already suggested, may also be a factor in the relationship of crowding to aggression. In studies of the effects of crowding on small groups, Freedman and his associates (1972) recruited 136 high school students (72 males and 64 females) and divided them into groups of eight subjects of the same sex. Each group was then split, with four subjects assigned to a very small room (with about 6 square feet per person) and four assigned to a larger room (where each person had about 20 square feet of space).

Each group of four spent several hours in the room, getting to know one another, and then was asked to play a simple game called the Prisoner's Dilemma, which can be played either cooperatively or competitively. In the Prisoner's Dilemma, a group that chooses to play cooperatively can be assured of winning four dollars apiece. The rules, however, allow players to compete with each other in the chance that one individual can win a large amount and the certainty that the group as a whole will win less—and in some instances will lose quite a lot. Competition in this game is clearly a somewhat aggressive strategy.

The one significant result of the study was that boys assigned to the small room played more competitively than did boys in the large room, which suggests that high density may have influenced this particular form of aggression. Surprisingly, girls seemed to respond in an opposite direction, showing more cooperation in the small room than in the large one.

In a second experiment, the same investigators used entirely different subjects in another city. These were 258 men and women ranging in age from 18 to 80, and representing almost the full spectrum of economic, occupational, and ethnic backgrounds. The experimental situation was a mock jury trial in which groups of all men, all women, or both men and women were placed in large or small "courtrooms" where they listened to five taped "courtroom trials" and then issued verdicts and sentences. The "jurors" had about 12 square feet per person in the small room, and about 25 square feet apiece in the large room.

The results were similar to those obtained with the high school students: under crowded conditions, the all-male groups gave slightly more severe sentences (and thus could be considered slightly more aggressive). In contrast, the all-female groups gave more lenient sentences in the crowded room than they did in the uncrowded one.

When both males and females were grouped together, the effects of density seemed to disappear when measured for the group as a whole. In other words, mixed-sex groups showed no difference, as a group, between the severity of the sentences issued in a crowded room and the severity of in a less-crowded situation.

The surprise in this study was the apparent effect, upon males, of the presence of females in the group. In mixed-sex "juries," males were much less severe in their sentences than were men in the all-male groups. The experimenters call this result irrelevant to crowding, per se, but of possible importance to lawyers and those interested in the effects of sexual segregation (Freedman, 1975, p. 148).

Aside from these objective behavioral effects, Freedman and his colleagues report some interesting subjective reactions. For instance, males in the small room reported their "jury" experience as less pleasant. They also liked their fellow participants less, felt they were not so friendly, and judged them poorer jurors than did the men in the large room. On the other hand, females felt just the opposite. They perceived the crowded experience as more pleasant, the other subjects as more likeable and more friendly. They also considered their companions better jurors under close-packed conditions than in more spacious surroundings. (No such significant differences were observed in the mixed-sex groups.)

From these experiments, at least, it seems clear that males tend to respond more negatively in high-density situations than do females, who seem to respond more positively under crowded conditions. Freedman et al. offer several hypotheses to explain these effects. They suggest that:

1. Males require more territory or space than do females, a characteristic that is innate.

2. Adult males are physically more active and larger than females and therefore require more space, or at least feel less comfortable when physical space is limited.

3. Close physical contact is not so acceptable among males as it is among females, a function of learned expectations about personal contact.

4. A crowded situation is likely to intensify subjective perceptions about being in a group of the same sex.

Since females (the authors suggest) are generally more relaxed in close proximity to each other, they will feel more comfortable in a group than will males, who generally perceive a group of men as threatening and antagonistic.

Perhaps the most interesting finding of the study is the possible "ameliorative" influence of women upon men. How, we cannot but wonder, will the presence of female sailors aboard ship affect the brawling tendencies of seamen? Are male residents of co-ed dormitories better behaved than those in all-male living situations? Is the tendency of males to become more aggressive in small quarters somehow linked to the absence of women? Or are the observations of Freedman and his colleagues simply isolated events?

Fortunately for the future of the debate over sex roles, there is another study with conclusions that contrast sharply with Freedman's. This is an experiment by Loo (1972), who watched 60 normal four- and five-year-old children at free play under low-density and high-density conditions. The subjects in this study served as their own control groups by experiencing both density conditions: 44 square feet per child and 15 square feet per child. The measured variables were *aggression* (defined as physically attacking a person or toy or causing discomfort to another person in any way) and *dominance* (defined as behaving in a controlling manner or imposing one's will on another).

The results, as we have hinted, are at variance with some of the expectations raised by Freedman's work. Male children in Loo's study showed significantly *less* aggressive behavior in the crowded space than they did in the less crowded area, while females showed about the same amount of aggression in both situations. Or, put the other way around, boys became significantly *more aggressive* under low-density conditions than they did under high density, while girls showed *no decrease* in aggression when crowded.

Another interesting finding is Loo's observation that boys showed no differences in their dominance ratings in the two situations, but that girls showed significantly more dominant behavior in the high-density setting than they did when less crowded.

Although Loo does not suggest a reason for the increased dominance of girls under crowded conditions, she explains her observations about aggression in this way:

> It appeared that aggression was encouraged by aggressive toys, by spatial conditions that allow enough room to attack and retreat, and by high excitation level. The high-density condition made gross motor activity difficult or else uncomfortable. It is quite possible, then, that restriction on movement discouraged the use of certain aggressive toys. We may be witnessing evidence that children adopt their play to the physical requirements of their environment (p. 379).

Another of Loo's observations deserves some discussion: the fact that in the high-density situation, many children chose to play by themselves. Could this be a response to too many stimuli, or the "autonomy" reaction Galle observed among Chicagoans who lived under severe conditions of "interpersonal press?" Or were these children merely sensitive to another spatial concept, the idea of "personal space" or the body-buffer zone into which no one intrudes without risk?

BODY-BUFFER ZONES, PERSONAL SPACE, AND HUMAN TERRITORIALITY

When we speak of keeping someone at "arm's length," we are expressing the idea that each person is surrounded by a sensitive spatial area into which few can enter without trespassing. For some people, "arm's length" is much too close.

Invasion of "personal space" usually raises the occupant's anxiety, sometimes to violent extremes. One psychiatrist (Kinzel, 1970) suggests that for some prison inmates, mere physical proximity was "at least as powerful a trigger of violence as were threats, thefts, or other more overt provocations."

Kinzel's conclusion is the result of a study in which he compared the body-buffer zones of violent and nonviolent prisoners and found that the violent group had buffer zones approximately four times as large as the nonviolent group. (This sensitivity to approach is related to aggression in that it's believed that violent prisoners sensing an intrusion on their "personal space" are likely to lash out or be provoked to violence.)

The eight violent prisoners chosen for the study had a history of "repeated violent behavior with little provocation, frequent necessity for forcible restraint, the use of weapons in fights, serious self-perpetuated accidents, bisexual and hypersexual behavior, hypersensitivity to name-calling, and a history of violence to domestic animals." They often reported a history of violence between their parents. In contrasts, the nonviolent prisoners had few of these characteristics.

Kinzel measured the prisoner's body-buffer zones by having each man stand in the center of a bare room while the experimenter walked toward him, and to say "Stop" when he felt the experimenter had come too close. (One prisoner said nothing, but clenched his fists and stalked away whenever the experimenter came too close.) Kinzel approached each man in this way from eight different directions, recorded the distances at which the subject said "Stop," and used these to calculate the area of each prisoner's buffer zone. He found that the average zone area for the violent prisoners was 29.3 square feet, while the nonviolent prisoners' zones averaged 7.0 square feet.

Kinzel suggests that violent individuals are much more likely to perceive intrusions into their space as potential attacks or as intrusions into their own bodies. And, he reports, these hypersensitive buffer zones are not easily dissolved. They appear to be instinctually linked to the violent prisoners' behavior. Even after twelve weeks of experiments, when they recognized the "intruder" as more of a friend than a foe, many of the prisoners maintained unusually large buffer zones. These findings emphasize the possibility that for persons already prone to violence, crowding may have very serious consequences.

Three other researchers (Hildreth, Derogatis, and McCusker, 1971) attempted to replicate and expand Kinzel's study of personal space and its relationship to aggression. They hypothesized that not only would violent inmates have larger body-buffer zones than nonviolent inmates also that but they would be more sensitive to people approaching from the rear than from the front, possibly interpreting such approach as a "sneak attack" on their personal space.

These investigators used two measures of aggression: one inferential, based on the concept of personal space; the other based on past history. To obtain the first measure, they used a technique similar to Kinzel's, approaching the subject from four different angles until he said "Stop." The second measure of aggression was based on a clinical impression from an interview as well as indications of violent behavior from a search of the case record. The results of this study confirmed those of Kinzel with one basic difference. While Kinzel reported that violent prisoners tended to have larger rear buffer zones and nonviolent prisoners tended to have larger front buffer zones, Hildreth and his associates found both the aggressive and the non-aggressive groups to be more sensitive to approach from the rear.

The authors account for these results by suggesting that most prison inmates possess homosexual anxiety or are at least fearful of being attacked from the rear.

Their general conclusion is that for humans, as well as for other animals, close physical proximity may be significantly related to intraspecies aggression.

The concept of personal space, or the idea that people have invisible and portable boundaries, seems to be linked to the basic phenomenon of territoriality. Territory differs from personal space in that territories have recognizable markers to indicate to others that they may be trespassing. Many ethologists argue that humans and animals handle space similarly in that both mark their territories (Ardrey, 1966; Hall, 1966; Lorenz, 1966). Bears, for example, mark their territories by clawing bark from trees, wolves urinate at the boundaries of their territories, and deer secrete a glandular substance that gives off an odor easily identified by other deer. People mark territories by fencing in their properties, putting up "no trespassing" signs, or placing books, sweaters, or coats on tables or chairs to indicate that the space is at least temporily taken. Generally, such fences or signs are effective. When they are disregarded, however, aggression and violence often result, with territorial disputes becoming more common as areas grow crowded.

For animals, the size of a marked territory is related to the amount of space needed for family growth or an adequate food supply, as well as the amount of space that can actually be defended. Humans have also used this logic in marking off their territories. For example, the old three-mile territorial coastal limit was based on the idea that the waters were needed for domestic fishing grounds, as well as the realization that only three miles of water could be adequately defended by coastal artillery. With growing populations and more sophisticated weaponry, territorial coastal limits have expanded considerably (to 200 miles in the case of the United States), and with them, the possibilities for violence in the event of intrusion. Even the vast oceans of the world seem to be suffering the effects of crowding.

But, whether international or local, is crowding really bad? Is it directly related to aggression or violence? To say (categorically) that it is not would be to ignore the evidence.

The fierce territoriality of birds, deer, and monkeys is well documented, as is the territoriality of *Homo sapiens* as evidenced by the countless bloody border disputes that punctuate human history.

We have seen demonstrations that crowding produces pathological behavior in rats, with physical aggression a common occurrence when the rats' environment degenerates into a behavioral sink.

There is evidence, too, that human environments become behavioral sinks, when cities are densely populated and people lack privacy, essential goods and services, or the reassurance of appropriate architectural designs. Statistics show higher crime rates and more juvenile delinquency among people living in these crowded areas.

Still, aggression in humans seems directed more at property than at people. Unlike rats, overcrowded, frustrated humans appear more interested in doing violence to each other's property or to the environment in general than to each other, a type of displacement activity we have seen elsewhere in the animal kingdom, among roe deer and herring gulls, for instance.

Perhaps it is possible for humans to carry such displacement activity one step further and to channel their aggressive energies into constructive or even creative pursuits. Winston Churchill, let's remember, was fond of "attacking" his canvases, perhaps with as much energy as he rallied to attack Britain's enemies.

But regardless of how well humans learn to sublimate their aggressive tendencies, each person still requires a certain amount of personal space in order to feel comfortable. Space, after all, is a fundamental ingredient of every entity and function in the universe. And nothing—from the smallest atom to the widest solar system—can maintain its identity or functional integrity without it. A given species can almost be defined by the space it occupies. Crowding might not destroy humanity, but it does influence us and must certainly change us.

It is hoped that with this knowledge we humans will not allow planet Earth to become a single, vast behavioral sink or an aggression-blasted radioactive particle drifting listlessly through the cosmos but will find ways to give each of us the personal space that means peace.

Crowding and Health

Chapter 8

Most of us feel that to avoid illness we should stay warm, eat properly, get plenty of rest, and *stay out of crowds.* When we don't follow this folk wisdom, we sometimes reap the results: a case of whatever "bug" is currently making the rounds. But if we tried to determine just why we had "caught the bug," where would we lay the blame? On cold, improper diet, fatigue, the "bug" itself, the crowd in which we "caught it," or upon some other factor entirely?

The traditional view of the link between crowding and health is straightforward: Crowding increases the opportunities for infection and seems to increase the likelihood of mortality from other causes as well. There are many reasons to believe this explanation, among them animal studies (such as Calhoun's described in the last chapter) that show higher death rates among crowded animals, reports of high human mortality in crowded urban areas, and records of frequent epidemics in densely populated living units such as military training camps, nurseries, and schools.

But valid as it may sound, the traditional view of crowding and health does little to help us understand today's epidemics of non-infectious illnesses, such as heart disease, arthritis, and cancer, nor does it adequately account for what we now know about infectious disease.

INFECTIVITY

According to the microbiologist René Dubos (1965), we do not actually "catch" most infectious illnesses, for the commonest microbial diseases arise from the activities of microorganisms that are everywhere in the environment, ordinarily existing in the body without causing harm. Most microbial disease does not result from exposure to new microorganisms but from disturbances in the balance between organisms and their hosts. Suggests Dubos: "In such a type of microbial disease the event of infection is of less importance than the hidden manifestation of the smoldering infectious process and the physiological disturbances that convert latent infection into overt symptoms and pathology."

Can crowding play a part in such physiological disturbance? It appears that although it can, its role is neither clear-cut nor direct and that considerable investigation must be done before we can completely understand it. Fortunately for researchers in this field, there are ready-made laboratories for the study of the relationship of crowding to disease—the military training camps, where outbreaks of infectious illness occur on a regular basis. According to one researcher (Cassel, 1971), the commonest recent cause of upper respiratory infection among closely-packed military recruits has been the adenovirus IV. And yet, this same microorganism is also widespread among civilian populations, where even in crowded colleges and schools it has never been implicated in the outbreak of upper respiratory infection. In addition, the permanent staffs of military training camps are not involved in the outbreaks, even though they live under the same crowded conditions as the recruits. If adenovirus IV causes a "disease of crowding," it evidently causes a selective one that afflicts only crowded recruits.

To further complicate our understanding of the "recruits' disease," Cassel reports that when immunization experiments against adenovirus IV were attempted in military camps, the immunized companies did have fewer cases of adenovirus IV, *but they experienced just as much upper respiratory illness as did the control companies.* Now, however, the recruits' illness was caused by a different agent—adenovirus VII!

Other studies (Stewart and Voors, 1968) of such outbreaks among Marine recruits at Parris Island, South Carolina, also suggest some kind of selectivity in the occurrence of illness. Stewart and Voors' study covered several eight-week stints of the Marines' basic training program, during which time the number of upper respiratory infections ordinarily increases from the first week through the fourth week, decreases in the fifth and sixth weeks, and begins to increase again in the seventh and eighth weeks. As far as the researchers could determine, there is no difference in the degree to which the recruits are crowded from one week to the next. Not only do upper respiratory infections follow a week-to-week pattern independent of changes in crowding, but sick calls from all causes follow the same pattern.

The Parris Island study also found systematic differences in infection rates from one platoon to another. Even though all the platoons lived under identical conditions, some had markedly higher infection rates for the entire eight weeks. As it can be assumed that a large percentage of the recruits were already harboring the ubiquitous virus when they began their training, it appears that they became ill not from "catching a bug" but rather because something in the military environment—or a particular platoon within that environment—led to the kind of physiological stress that converts latent infection into overt symptoms.

In Chapter 4 we mentioned a study by McCain et al. (1976) of crowding in prisons. The researchers studied reports about prison inmates who had lived a minimum of 30 days in either a dormitory (with 26 or more men) or a single or two-man cell. For each man, a detailed housing and medical history was compiled, covering a minimum of six months prior to the investigation. Then, for five weeks, the researchers kept track of the "kites" (or written requests for medical attention) submitted by the inmates.

At the end of five weeks, a comparison of "kites" from the different groups showed that the men in the dormitory had a significantly higher illness complaint rate than the men in the single or two-man cells. The most frequent complaints were of back pain, nausea, rash, sinus problems, constipation, chest pain, and asthma. (Complaints of colds, flu, or traumatic injuries such as bone fractures were not construed as being related to stress and thus were not counted in this study.)

The investigators conceded the possibility that the higher complaint rate from the dormitory might be as much a reflection of length of imprisonment as of type of housing, because in the prison they studied, inmates are initially housed in dormitories and later transferred to single or two-man cells. To explore this possibility, they compared "kite" rates for new inmates during their first 30 days as well as their last 14 to 30 days in the dormitory. Their reasoning was that if complaint rates really did decline in proportion to the length of the inmates' imprisonment, there would be a lower complaint rate during the last 14 to 30 days of dormitory housing. McCain et al. found no such difference. This led them to suggest that inmates in single and two-man cells complain less of illness partly because of their housing conditions and that "high social density and/or spatial density induces stress that, like other stressors, can increase the rate of illness complaints" (p. 287).

When the same investigators conducted a similar study in a county jail, where crowding was more intense than in the prison facility, they again found a significantly greater rate of illness complaints filed by men in the more crowded units.

Whether or not the stress of crowded imprisonment led to actual illness or merely to "illness complaints" in this study might be argued. But the fact that imprisonment under crowded conditions leads to some kind of physiologically experienced stress seems undeniable.

HYPERTENSION

For a better understanding of the physiological effects of stress, there is probably no better area to explore than hypertension, or high blood pressure—the current leader among chronic diseases in humans. In recent years, a number of researchers have set out to explore the circumstances in which hypertension occurs as well as the mechanisms that bring it about. In a 1967 animal study, Henry et al. found that they could induce prolonged hypertension in mice by subjecting the animals to a variety of "psychosocial stimuli," including crowding. The stimuli consisted of mixing animals previously housed in different boxes, aggregating mice in small boxes, subjecting groups of mice to a predator, and inducing conflict for territory by placing equal numbers of males and females in an interconnecting box system.

Under the most stressful of these circumstances, the mean arterial blood pressure of the mice rose from 126 mm/Hg to the range of 150-160 mm/Hg and was sustained at this level for six to nine months. It is interesting to note that these changes were most marked in mice that had previously led uncrowded lives. Animals which had been aggregated since birth showed a lesser degree of blood pressure elevation.

In a later experiment, Henry et al. (1971) were able to pinpoint the mechanism that produced hypertension in the mice. Somewhat simplified, the mechanism is as follows: "psychosocial stimulation" increases the rate at which the adrenal medulla produces two enzymes, tyrosine hydroxylase and phenylethanolamine-N-transferase (PNMT), that are involved in the synthesis and metabolism of two hormones known to affect blood pressure. These "stress hormones," noradrenaline and adrenaline, are also called catecholamines. In the socially stimulated mice, the researchers found increases not only in the formation of catecholamines but also in the weight of the adrenal gland and the animals blood pressure.

Unlike the sudden temporary discharge of catecholamines produced by anger or the threat of aggression—a phenomenon with strong survival value in the wild—these psychosocially stimulated enzyme responses take several hours to develop and are evidently the result of long-sustained adrenal medullary responses to acute social stimulation. Such prolonged catecholamine production is thought to result in sustained elevation of blood pressure (as was seen in the mice) and in subsequent damage to organs such as the brain, heart, and kidneys.

In other words, mice who care about their health would do well to avoid prolonged psychosocial stress. Should the same caution be heeded by humans? The question is worth serious attention, for a similar increase in "stress hormone" formation has been observed in humans under the "psychosocially stimulating" conditions of crowding.

A human study (Lundberg, 1976) was carried out with male Swedish commuters, all regular morning passengers on a train between Nynäshamn and Stockholm. One group of subjects regularly boarded the train at the start of the trip; the others got on about halfway through the 72-minute journey to Stockholm. The researchers asked the passengers to rate their subjective experiences at different points along the way and then to donate three urine samples to be analyzed for catecholamines: the first after a "normal" train trip, the second after a more crowded train trip during a brief period of gas rationing, and the third in a control condition at home.

Lundberg reports the following results from the study:

1. On both train trips, the subjects reported that "unpleasantness" increased and "comfort" decreased as the train became progressively more crowded at each stop along the way to Stockholm. These negative reactions were intensified during the second trip, when the train was more crowded than usual (even though seats were available for most passengers on both trips). Even though the second train carried only 10 percent more passengers than the first, the commuters in the study reported a significantly higher degree of "perceived crowdedness."

2. Urinalyses showed that on both trips, subjects who boarded the train halfway to Stockholm, when it was already quite full, had higher levels of both adrenaline and noradrenaline in their urine than did the men who got on at the start of the trip.

3. On the second, more crowded trip, both groups of subjects had higher levels of adrenaline in their urine than they did under control conditions.

To Lundberg, these findings suggest that:

The "stress" resulting from a train journey depends more on the conditions on the train than upon the duration or length of the journey itself, at least within certain limits. The degree of control over the situation on the train, such as the possibility of choosing seats and company, was assumed to be of significant importance for reducing the stress involved. . . . The catecholamine data show that differences in travelling conditions for the subjects from Nynäshamn [the beginning of the trip] and Västerhaninge [the halfway point] were reflected in both adrenaline and noradrenaline excretion. As the travelling conditions were identical for the two groups during the second part of the trip (Västerhaninge to Stockholm) the lower mean excretion rate of the Nynäshamn subjects probably was related to their travelling conditions during the first part of the trip. . . . They boarded an empty train and were, thus, able to choose seats and company very freely (p. 31).

Lundberg found it especially interesting that a relatively small difference in the number of passengers per car between the two trips was associated with a much larger difference in perceived crowdedness and also a significant difference in physiological arousal as measured by the output of stress hormones.

If the stress of mild crowding for brief periods under fairly comfortable circumstances can produce measurable physiological changes in humans, what kinds of changes occur in people who must remain in crowded conditions for long periods of time? This, basically, was the question posed by two American researchers (D'Atri and Ostfeld, 1973) when they studied the blood pressure and pulse rates of male prison inmates who lived in single cells, shared cells, and large dormitories in three separate institutions. (They also collected demographic and subcultural data on each inmate, along with information on personal characteristics, height, weight, education, previous occupation, confinement history, smoking history, attitude of guards, and the subjects' attitudes about the size and crowdedness of the institution.)

D'Atri and Ostfeld found that, in Prison A, black and white

prisoners in dormitories had higher blood pressures (both systolic and diastolic) than did the men who occupied single or double cells. They found a similar situation in Prison B, where black and white dormitory dwellers averaged significantly higher blood pressures than white inmates in single cells. In Prison C, white inmates in dormitories had higher overall blood pressures than white inmates in single cells. (Black dormitory dwellers in Prison C had higher systolic pressures than did black prisoners in single cells, but the relationship did not apply to diastolic pressures.) In Prison C, pulse rates were higher among black and white dormitory residents than among black and white residents of single cells.

The researchers believe these results strongly support their major hypothesis that there would be an association between degree of crowding and blood pressure. Writes D'Atri (1975):

> Crowding, however . . . is not simple expression of number of square feet of floor space per inmate, [since some of the men in single cells had no more square feet of space allocated to them than the men in dormitories]. . . . Rather, crowding is a multidimensionality incorporating physical, social, and personal variables. Men in dormitories have a much greater likelihood of threatening interpersonal relations, including assault by prisoners, threats by guards, homosexual rape, and conflicts over territoriality . . . (p. 249).

D'Atri (1975) also found an interesting (although not statistically significant) association between the inmates' reports of degree of crowding, their attitudes toward their guards, and blood pressure levels:

> Those inmates (in particular the white ones) viewing the environment as crowded and the guards as harsh tended to have higher pressures. An interesting exception . . . is that those who view the guards as "very easygoing" have higher pressures than all groups except the one viewing the guards as "very harsh." Psychiatric theory may explain this seeming discrepancy, i.e., those who report the guards as very easygoing may be those very repressors of aggressive feelings who are believed to have higher blood pressure (p. 247).

D'Atri also notes an interesting association between the duration of confinement and the rise in blood pressure. "This time trend suggests the operation of two factors on blood pressures during confinement: one, a factor of anxiety or novelty during the first two weeks in jail, and then another factor, probably related to crowding, beginning after a month's confinement and having a progressive effect thereafter in elevating pressures (p. 247)."

In view of these findings, D'Atri points out the irony that prison dormitories are often considered "preferential housing," when, in fact, their physiological effects upon prisoners may be very negative.

Most of us are fortunate enough not to live under the kind of intense stress experienced by crowded prison inmates, and yet all of us experience psychosocial stress of some kind. What is it that makes some people better able to handle it than others? Why do some people become ill under stress-producing circumstances, while others seem to thrive on constant, complex social interactions? A partial explanation may lie in the adaptability of the human organism, a phenomenon that may contain the key to urban survival.

ADAPTATION—THE KEY TO URBAN SURVIVAL?

In his 1971 study of the health consequences of population and crowding, Cassel points out that prior to 1950, death rates from all causes in the United States were higher in urban areas than in rural areas, but that by 1960, this ratio had been reversed, with rural death rates higher than urban. Since 1960, even though cities have continued to grow larger and more crowded, rural death rates have continued to increase in comparison with urban death rates.

Part of this phenomenon can certainly be attributed to the better medical care and sanitation of the cities and part to the migration of younger people to urban areas, leaving older, more susceptible population behind in the country. But, Cassel says, these facts only partially explain the reversal of the rural-urban health ratio. Improved urban sanitation and medical care may explain why rural populations have higher death rates from typhoid fever, for example, and the immunization programs in cities probably account for the lower urban rates of diptheria and pertussis. But neither factor explains why more people get scarlet fever in the country, as there is, as yet, no known way to prevent the occurrence of streptococcal infections in either environment. Similarly, says Cassel, the migration of the young to the cities does not explain the higher mortality rates among rural children.

This reversal of the traditional urban-rural health ratio can perhaps be seen most clearly in the example of tuberculosis, a disease that increased rapidly in most cities as they became industrialized and crowded. After increasing for 75 to 100 years following industrialization, however, TB rates then began falling spontaneously and have continued to fall in spite of continuing increases in population density. As this decrease began in the U.S. and Britain some 50 to 100 years before the discovery of any useful antituberculosis drugs, and decades before the beginning of the first antituberculosis programs, modern medical care can hardly account for the trend.

Other diseases that have increased, then peaked and declined as populations have grown in the U.S. and Britain include the malnutrition syndromes of rickets and pellagra, early childhood diseases, and duodenal ulcer, which, during the time between the first and second World Wars, grew to epidemic proportions, especially in young men.

Today, duodenal ulcer seems to be on the wane, replaced by the "modern" epidemics of coronary heart disease, hypertension, cancer, arthritis, diabetes, and mental disorders. According to Cassel, some of these illnesses may also have peaked and begun their decline—undoubtedly to be replaced by new "diseases of civilization."

How can we account for such phenomena, which seem to occur somewhat independently of advances in medical care? A partial explanation seems to lie in the ability of organisms to adapt to a wide range of conditions, including the stresses of crowding. A number of animal studies such as the one done by Henry et al. (1967) indicate that mice born and reared in populations of extreme density do not show the same physiological reactions as did their progenitors, to whom the stresses of crowding had been new and unfamiliar.

Support for this idea of organismic adaptation comes from an American study of managers (cited by Cassel, 1971) in which it was found that managers who had completed college suffered considerably less illness than did nongraduate managers doing the same job for the same pay in the same company. The college graduates in the survey were almost entirely fourth-generation Americans, sons of managers, proprietors, or white-collar workers who had grown up in middle-to high-income families in "good neighborhoods." The nongraduate group, originally hired as skilled craftsmen, had later advanced to managerial status. These men were the sons and grandsons of immigrants, whose fathers had been skilled or unskilled laborers with an average of grammar school education or less. They had grown up in low-income families in modest to substandard neighborhoods.

Cassel suggests that this latter group suffered significantly more illnesses of all sorts than did the first group partly because they were less well-prepared for the demands and expectations of their managerial status.

Cassel and Tyroler (1961) came to a similar conclusion following their study of two groups of rural mountaineers, one composed of people who were the first of their family ever to engage in industrial work and the second of workers in the same factory, from the same mountain areas, who were children of previous workers in the factory. As predicted, the investigators found that the sons of previous factory workers had fewer symptoms of illness and lower rates of sick absenteeism than the "first generation" workers—a fact that suggests that the "second generation" workers were better prepared for, or adapted to, their industrial roles.

Another factor that seems to afford individuals some protection against illness is membership in a stable group. Numerous studies cited by Cassel (1971) have shown that members of small, cohesive societies such as those found in parts of Africa and the Pacific Islands tend to have low blood pressures that do not differ between the young and the aged. Several of these studies have followed some of these people as they left their own cultures to become residents of Western cities. As newcomers in their urban settings, the subjects were found to have higher blood pressures than did their kinfolk back home. They also displayed the familiar relationship between blood pressure and age that shows up in Western populations.

A British investigation of tuberculosis also supports the idea that group or family members may enjoy better health than do "social isolates." In this study (Brett and Benjamin, 1957), all the people in a city were X-rayed for signs of tuberculosis. The results showed that lodgers living in single rooms had a TB rate three to four times as high as that of family members.

A similar situation was reported by a U.S. researcher (Holmes, 1956), who found that TB occurred most frequently among "marginal" Seattle residents, those who lack meaningful social contact. Among the people with higher than average rates of the disease were those representing ethnic minorities in their neighborhoods, people living alone in one room, people who had frequently changed occupation or residence, and single or divorced persons. Cassel (1971) also reports that higher than average rates of respiratory disease other than tuberculosis, as well as schizophrenia, accidents, and suicides, have been found among people who, for one reason or another, might be classified as "outsiders," or the lonely ones in the crowd. All these people might be considered to be suffering from the urban phenomenon of "atomization" of the groups that provide emotional support and possibly health protection for people in smaller societies.

But it would be a mistake to suggest that "group membership," in itself, confers on all the members some kind of immunity to stress. In animal experiments (Welch, 1964, Mason, 1965) it was found that animals who occupied subordinate roles in a group "pecking order," or hierarchy, reacted in a far more extreme way to standardized stimuli than did animals in dominant roles. Some of the responses of the subordinate animals included changes in the endocrine secretions as well as outright examples of disease and pathology.

No equivalent research has been carried out among humans, but the previously mentioned studies of illness among military trainees and blood pressure in prisoners suggest that "pecking order" might also be a factor in human physiological responses to crowding.

Everything we have considered so far points up the fact that the relationship between crowding and health is extremely complex. Social density and crowding do appear to be connected to health issues, but not in the way they were once thought to be. Rather than acting directly to cause infection or other illness, crowding seems to operate indirectly, serving as a catalyst in various physiological processes. By increasing the number of social interactions (both voluntary and involuntary) between people, crowding heightens the importance of the social environment as a factor in physiological response. It also increases the importance of the *quality* of our social environment; for our perceptions of it as "pleasant," "unpleasant," "stressful," "soothing," "hostile," "supportive," or just plain "crowded" seem to influence our bodily reactions to it.

We have seen evidence, for instance, that crowded commuters may experience less stress when they feel they have at least the freedom to choose their own seats and companions. It has been postulated that city dwellers enjoy better health when they belong to families or other support groups, and that urban newcomers— who often lack such supports—are particularly vulnerable to illness.

The relationship between crowding and health may be better expressed as an interaction between privacy and health. When one achieves a level of social interaction that is consistent and comfortable then he has achieved a desired or healthy level of privacy. However as Altman (1975) suggests "if achieved privacy is lower or higher than desired privacy—too much or little contact—a state of imbalance exists" (p. 10).

In the next and final chapter we examine in more depth what we believe to be the essence of the psychology of crowding, that is, the desire for privacy.

Privacy

Chapter 9

Give me, kind Heaven, a private station, A mind serene for contemplation.—John Gay

"Love or perish" we are told and we tell ourselves. The phrase is true enough so long as we don't interpret it as "Mingle or be a failure." Loving our neighbor should not mean that we must sit in his lap.
                                                                    —Phyllis McGinley

When, about 40 years ago, Swedish film star Greta Garbo insisted, "I want to be alone," she shocked a world not easily shocked by the eccentricities of anyone in the movie realm. A beautiful, talented woman, but decidedly peculiar—as peculiar perhaps as the "problem" child who preferred to sit in his or her room and read. The loner was someone to weep for, and to rehabilitate. It was often not understood that loneliness and aloneness are different, that being lonely implies dejection caused a lack of love and attention, whereas being alone is a means of renewing the self and even sometimes reaching into a transcendental realm beyond the self.

Today Garbo's remark, far from making headlines, would be

regarded as eminently sensible. The increasingly complex society and plethora of people spawned during the last four decades have intensified the harshness, stimuli, and crush of the modern world, particularly in the cities. For many people the sense of being hemmed in has become overwhelming. They want, occasionally at least, to be free of terrorism, murky air, sleazy streets, transistor radios, mass advertising, junk mail, smelly traffic, long lines, jackhammers, and jet engines. They are appalled by and feel helpless to evade a surveillance technology whose tentacles have wormed into their private lives. They need a respite from social observations and social assumptions, from the daily masquerade. As Eiseley (1971) puts it, "The fact is that many of us who walk to and fro upon our usual tasks are prisoners drawing mental maps of escape" (p. 204).

PRIVACY AS A BASIC NEED

We tend to believe that the desire for privacy is singularly human, born of mankind's cultural evolution. But recent findings indicate that the search for privacy springs from our animal origins and that the devices used by both human beings and animals to achieve privacy are strikingly similar.

Temporary individual seclusion or the intimacy of a small group is sought by nearly all animals. By laying claim to a specific area and defending it against intrusion, an organism manifests what Robert Ardrey calls "the territorial imperative." (See Chapter 7) The robin's song and the monkey's shriek may therefore not be a display of the sheer "animal joy of life" but rather a defiant warning to possible intruders to stay out of private territory (Ardrey, 1971).

Both animals and humans also have elaborate mechanisms for regulating space. Hall (1966) describes these as "personal distance," which is established between noncontact animals (for instance, the spacing of birds on a telephone wire); "intimate distance," which is set up between mates or between parents and their offspring; and "social distance," which links the members of an animal group with one another while setting them off from other groups. Crowding apparently affects animals and human beings in much the same way, creating metabolic stress and possibly producing such diseases as heart ailments, hypertension, and circulatory diseases.

Finally, as Westin (1967) observes,

> Animals also need the stimulation of social encounters among their own species. As a result, the animal's struggle to achieve a balance between privacy and participation provides one of the basic processes of animal life. In this sense, the quest for privacy is not restricted to man alone, but arises in the biological and social processes of all life (pp. 10-11).

For the human being, this means that "We become what we are not only by establishing boundaries around ourselves but also by a periodic opening of these boundaries to nourishment, to learning, and to intimacy" (A. Simmel, 1971).

Although American norms of privacy are certainly not universal, virtually every society, whether it be primitive or modern, has ways of achieving privacy and of adjusting its values of disclosure and surveillance. In social interactions the individual is obliged to play different roles with different persons at different times. Murphy (1964) comments that to protect himself or herself from the stresses of this interaction, a person uses "reserve and restraint" to create "an area of privacy." This "common, though not constant" factor in every social relationship is one of the key "dialectical processes in social life." The avoidance rules and the techniques for setting distance are countless. They range from simple verbalizing, to body language, to facing a wall, to covering the face (the veils of Tuareg men, the fans used by women), to averting the eyes, to covering the eyes (as with the dark glasses used by VIPs in Latin America, the Near and Middle East, and the United States, though certainly not restricted to them).

THE PRIVILEGE OF PRIVACY

To nourish the inner life and to make intense affiliations bearable, privacy is not only a necessity but, ironically, also one of our greatest luxuries. Phyllis McGinley (1959), who has called the inventor of the door as great a benefactor to mankind as the person who discovered fire, notes:

> Out of the cave, the tribal tepee, the pueblo, the community fortress, man emerged to build himself a house of his own with a shelter in it for himself and his diversions. Every age has seen it so. The poor might have to huddle together in cities for need's sake, and the frontiersman cling to his neighbors for the sake of protection. But in each civilization, as it advanced, those who could afford it chose the luxury of a withdrawing-place. Egyptians planned vine-hung gardens, the Greeks had their porticos and seaside villas, the Romans put enclosures around their patios, and English gentlemen retired into their country seats guarded by parks and lime-walks and disciplined stone walls (p. 56).

If the achievement of privacy sometimes confers status, so does the ability to invade privacy. Schwartz (1968) suggests, for instance, that the prestige of the physician stems partially from his authority to disregard the barriers of privacy (p. 743). On the other hand, an individual of high status, prompted by the social invisibility of one of low status (a "nonperson," who offers no challenge to the selfhood of his or her superior), may not even bother to erect a barrier of privacy. Goffman (1973), for instance, quotes Mrs. Trollope on the habitual indifference of Americans to their servants in the mid-1800s:

> They talk of them, of their condition, of their faculties, of their conduct, exactly as if they were incapable of hearing. . . . A Virginian gentleman told me that ever since he had married, he had been accustomed to have a Negro girl sleep in the same chamber with himself and his wife. I asked for what purpose this nocturnal attendance

was necessary. "Good Heaven!" was the reply. "If I wanted a glass of water during the night, what would become of me?" (p. 152).

The social invisibility of others is sometimes assumed when two people lapse into a foreign language or when children start talking in pig-Latin. In these cases, however, if an eavesdropper happens to know the foreign language or be adept at pig-Latin, he or she can fake social invisibility and smugly listen to whatever secrets are being told.

CULTURAL VARIATIONS OF PRIVACY

When people travel abroad, they frequently experience "culture shock," because familiar cues are either removed or distorted and strange ones crop up in their stead. One of the outstanding ways in which cultures differ is in their use of space. Their different sensory worlds make for widely varied notions of privacy; and these are reflected in a people's architecture, furniture arrangement, use of public space, and setting of social distance.

Hall (1966) notes that the Germans express their need for *Lebensraum* by closed doors, at home and in the office, and by rigid rules regarding "trespass" in person-to-person relations. Their private territory encompasses a larger sphere than either Americans or the British deem necessary for comfort.

The British, traditionally less habituated to the use of doors, walls, and strict rules of trespass, achieve their privacy largely through reserve, (not, for example, feeling that they have to be neighborly just because someone lives nearby) and through speaking softly to discourage eavesdroppers. When an Englishman lapses into silence, it's a cue that he wants privacy. When an American does so, it may well be taken as a sign that something is wrong.

Mediterranean peoples, who enjoy packing closely together in public, are often regarded as "pushy" by Americans. On the other hand, while Americans will casually invite mere acquaintances into their homes, the French reserve their homes for family privacy and may let several years pass before opening them to a friend, if indeed they relent at all.

Latin Americans tend to feel uncomfortable talking to others unless they are so close that North Americans figure they are either hostile or sexually motivated. The result is that North Americans, who don't like people breathing down their necks or spraying their faces, back away or barricade themselves somehow, and the Latin Americans translate this as cold and unfriendly. So different are the sensory worlds that people of various cultures inhabit that what is respect for privacy in one is intrusion in another, a perfect situation for misunderstandings (Hall, 1959; Hall, 1966; Westin, 1967).

THE NATURE AND FUNCTIONS OF PRIVACY

Westin (1967, pp. 31-32) has neatly categorized individual privacy into four basic states:

1. Solitude, "the most complete state of privacy that individuals can achieve;"
2. Intimacy, without which "a basic need of human contact would not be met;"
3. Anonymity, which allows the individual "to merge into the 'situational landscape'" and be unafraid that strangers will exert authority or restraint over him or her.
4. Reserve, "the most subtle state of privacy" in which a psychological barrier against intrusion is erected by the individual and honored by others.

Although we spend most of our lives in intimate situations and group settings, we always, even in our most intimate relations, hold back some parts of ourselves "as either too personal and sacred or too shameful and profane to express" (Westin, 1967, p. 32). This, according, to George Simmel (1950) creates a tension between "self-revelation and self-restraint" within the individual, and between "trespass and discretion" within society.

The functions that privacy performs for each individual are essentially "personal autonomy, emotional release, self-evaluation, and limited and protected communication" (Westin, 1967, p. 32; see pp. 32-39 for an excellent analysis of these functions).

Each of us plays a number of roles in public, hiding behind a mask. It is privacy that allows us to be "off-stage," to take off our masks, to have a breather, to be ourselves. For to be always "on" would be to destroy ourselves. There are indeed some self-sacrificing, suffering individuals who find it immensely difficult to shed their masks even when alone, as if fearful of what Keats called "the desolation of reality." They actually believe themselves to be the "characters" they play in public, not realizing that it is necessary to be aware

> of the masquerades and deceptions that are part of good role performance . . . to recall ourselves to our *own* selfhood and to our opposition to that of others. We must indeed deceive others to be true to ourselves. . . . Daily life is . . . sparked by a constant tension between sincerity and guile, between self-release and self-containment, between the impulse to embrace that which is public and the drive to escape the discomfort of group demands. Accordingly, our identities are maintained by our ability to hold back as well as to affiliate (Schwartz, 1968, p. 752).

It is in reflective solitude that that the greatest creativity occurs. Although "brain-storming" has been touted as a royal route to brilliant ideas, studies have revealed that group-think sessions are quantitatively not as productive as periods of private, individual work by the same number of people. The creative imagination has ever flouished in solitude. In fact, according to Peter Viereck (1958), "in a free democracy the only justified aristocracy is that of the lonely creative bitterness, the artistically creative scars of the fight for the inner dimension against outer mechanization: the fight for the private life" (p. 14).

Through the enforced isolation of prison, societies have, for better or worse and however unintentionally, granted the privacy (or "the productive alienation") without which society-modifying works might never have been written. It was in prison, as Sisk (1975) points out, that Cervantes conceived *Don Quixote* and Sir Walter Raleigh wrote *History of the World.* And "prison afforded the privacy and reflection necessary for Thomas Malory's *Morte d'Arthur,* Bunyan's *Pilgrim's Progress,* Hitler's *Mein Kampf,* and Cleaver's *Soul on Ice.* Who more than the Marquis de Sade and Jean Genet are able to say, 'Prison made me'?" (p. 104). Obviously, for millions of prisoners and others forced to separate physically from society (e.g., disaster victims, explorers), too much isolation can, like too little privacy, gravely undermine an individual's well-being (Westin, 1967, p. 40). But it can be argued that isolation is not true privacy.

Whether our privacy is a privacy of dreams, of weeping, of emptiness, or of rebellion, it enables each of us to recharge ourselves, recast our thoughts, reinforce our uniqueness.

THE DESTRUCTION OF THE PRIVATE SELF

For perhaps too many years it has been fashionable to assume that a sense of personal identity and self-awareness can best come by opening up unreservedly to others, by generously sharing one's inner life. Keeping anything secret, personal, or private is, in this view, bad, if not downright pathological. The so-called uptight among us are encouraged to "let it all hang out": spilling guts and baring the soul is the only salvation. Many have been EST-ed and encounter-grouped and Gestalted out of their privacy—and, in some cases, out of their minds. As Cottle (1975a) describes it: "First go the clothes, then the easy feelings, then the tough feelings, then the secrets, and finally the entire inner self. When all this stuff has been exposed, we will supposedly be free, or equal, or open, or renewed, or something" (p. 22).

Those who regarded monogamous marriage as passé, or at least excessively private, recommend airing it out with swinging encounters with other couples, or orgies, or the enrichment of a third partner. And the androgynous and the anti-private are promoted, especially by the young, as unisex transcends heterosex (Sisk, 1975). As the urge to merge is accompanied by the urge to purge, it has reached the point where it is hard "to lose one's job or virginity, one's identity or sanity, one's health or loved ones, without writing a book about it" or discussing it on a talk show. "When we tell everything no one can control us." The paradox is that those who are "cool," silent, or reclusive are seen as a bit scary. Once they reveal themselves, it is felt, it will be possible to have some hold on them (Cottle, 1975b, pp. 19, 21).

The sponsors of all this indiscriminate togetherness (including those who have found the inner life a highly lucrative commodity) claim that it is marvelous for personal and mutual growth. They are not convincing. People must, of course, be able to free themselves from disturbing thoughts and emotions that jeopardize their own well-being and their relationships with others. But the need to divulge must be balanced by the need to withhold and protect. For example, although some school psychologists have begun diagnosing a new and serious childhood illness called shyness (which they sometimes treat with drugs to "open the children up"), psychiatrists and other behavioral scientists have recently found that anxious or difficult children need to be allowed to have secrets and unrevealed thoughts and a private environment. For "being able to have secrets gives us a sense of security" (Kira, 1973, p. 34).

THE PURSUIT OF PRIVACY

The one place Americans can generally still count on for privacy is the bathroom. As open living becomes more and more popular and the amount of space available in most people's residences shrinks, they are finding it increasingly difficult to locate other places to be alone. The upshot is that many people privatize public places, spending long hours in city streets, in libraries, in bus stations, in bars, in movie houses (Lofland, 1973). Some will go to extraordinary lengths to be alone, even spending some $10 an hour to cocoon themselves in a Lilly Tank. This womb of one's own is a self-enclosed structure containing 10 inches of saltwater heated to 93 degrees and completely shielding the occupant from the world outside.

The mushrooming spiritual movement is, in part at least, a manifestation of the quest for more privacy. The same is true of jogging, which for some is not the loneliness of the long-distance runner but a chance to be free and more aware—and private.

And, finally, an enormous number of wandering Americans, as many as 30 million, have simply turned their backs on old values and opted out—living from day to day, uninvolved and unattached. These restless ones don't work steadily, don't join community groups, don't vote, don't settle, and reportedly don't read. It is not clear whether this new Lost Generation is searching for its soul, but if it is indeed searching for more privacy, it is probably having more success than the rest of us.

APARTNESS FOR TOGETHERNESS

Privacy—"the boldness of self-space" (Raines, 1974, p. 113)—is, in the final analysis, a matter of reciprocity. Narcissistic or unproductive privacy assumes that everybody and everything external to the self is of value only if they lead to self-enhancement. Productive privacy, on the other hand, assumes that the whole is greater than the sum of its parts, so that what comes out of that privacy is good not just for the individual but, somehow, for the whole community. "Privacy," writes Sisk (1975), "is a community thing, whether in marriage or in the larger social units" (p. 102).

Although Kahlil Gibran (1966, pp. 15-16) was writing of marriage when he penned the following lines, he also expressed for us, indelibly, the essence of privacy:

. . . Let there be spaces in your togetherness, And let the winds of the heavens dance between you. Love one another, but make not a bond of love. . . . Sing and dance together and be joyous, But let each one of you be alone, Even as the strings of a lute are alone though they quiver with the same music. *

*Reprinted from THE PROPHET, by Kahlil Gibran, with permission from the publisher, Alfred A. Knopf, Inc. Copyright 1923 by Kahlil Gabran; renewal copyright by Administrators C.T.A. of Kahlil Gabran Estate, and Mary G. Gibran.

Epilogue

During the early 1800s, when slave trade was at its peak, an economic controversy arose among slave traders concerning the best way to transport slaves from one continent to another. The "tight packers" claimed that although a crowded ship had more fatalities than a loosely packed ship, more profits could be realized with a tightly packed ship because there were more slaves to sell. The "loose packers," on the other hand, felt that it was economically advantageous to give the slaves some space on a long voyage since the slaves would be more likely to survive in a less crowded ship and would be in better condition when they arrived at their destination. According to an economic analysis of this situation made in the 1850s, the loose packers' strategy was more economically sound and in the long run yielded the highest profits.

The inhuman physical conditions forced on slaves in transporting them for trade provided a natural setting and population for studying the effects of crowding. Of course, variables other than crowding contributed to the high mortality rates aboard the "slavers"— the loss of roots and severed family ties in particular. Nevertheless, the differential in mortality rates between the overcrowded and less crowded ships suggests that the effects of crowding contributed significantly to whether one lived or died on these long voyages.

Unfortunately, natural settings have seldom been used by investigators to study the effects of crowding. In any event, there are no parallels to crowded slave ships among the culture-bound studies of crowding conducted by social psychologists. Most of their experiments define the crowded setting in terms of a small room occupied by five or more people performing a learning task. The time spent in the room rarely exceeds several hours. No one has to elbow his way from one side of the room to the other merely to get a glass of water. On experimenter, for example, arranged varying amounts of space (35, 80, and 160 square feet) for five to nine people and measured their ability to perform a learning task under these varying conditions of density. As one might expect, he found no differences among these groups in their ability to learn these performance tasks and concluded that crowding has no effects on learning. Clearly, this type of experiment is meaningless in practical terms because it cannot account for the fact that most people feel the stress of crowding only when they have to compete for limited space. At the very least, this should involve physically moving around and coping with other people—a condition seldom used by investigators into the effects of crowding. To successfully predict the long-term consequences of crowded environments it is essential that we study natural environments.

THE SOCIAL CLIMATE
OF DENSELY POPULATED ENVIRONMENTS

Environments that have dense populations differ in social climate from environments with sparse populations. The difference is especially marked in the crowded tenements of the poor. The person who has grown up in the city without experiencing the freedom of the open space of the countryside perceives fewer options in the way he relates to his world. Because his world has so many people in it and so many confusing stimuli, he puts greater social distance between himself and others. He copes with the social milieu by assigning stereotyped priorities to the people he encounters. The urbanite is more likely to respond to a stranger in trouble by thinking to himself, "I can't afford to get involved with this person" or else, without thinking at all, he assigns such situations a low enough priority so as to avoid the encounter altogether.

The person growing up in the small community or countryside has to cope with fewer social stimuli and tends to relate to his world on a more comfortable basis. He isn't required to process his environment so quickly to maintain his equilibrium. He places more positive value on interpersonal relationships. A helping orientation comes more easily to the small town dweller than to the urbanite.

CAN WE SURVIVE WITHOUT THE COUNTRYSIDE?

A totally urban life goes counter to human biology. Man has lived in an urban environment for only a tiny fraction of the total time he has been in existence. There has not been time enough to evolve mechanisms to cope successfully with high density living. We are inextricably tied to blue skies, trees, green grass, and vegetation. In some cities blue skies have become a rarity. The greyish-brown haze of smog is omnipresent, hanging continuously over the city.

Unfortunately, the urban population has a tendency toward panic and aggression when it has been excluded from or deprived of the countryside's open spaces. In ancient and medieval times, cities were walled in so that they could adequately defend themselves. In fact, the concept of cities and the posture of aggression are historically wedded to each other: cities with little or no open space have often been in a permanent state of siege. Cities with no land to grow vegetation instead are seed beds of pollution and frustration, leading to riots and violence.

The spread of urban areas portends an ominous future for the countryside. People spill over onto the green land, covering it with houses, streets, and concrete. Can we survive without the countryside and without space in which to find physical and psychological freedom? It is unlikely.

References

Chapter 1

GUMP, P.V., AND ROSS, R., Problems and possibilities in measurement of school environments. Unpublished paper, delivered at the Third Bienniel Conference of the International Society for the Study of Behavioural Development at the University of Surrey, Guildford, England, July, 1975.

Chapter 2

ALTMAN, I., *The Environment and Social Behavior.* Monterey, Calif.: Brooks/Cole, 1975.

ARDREY, R., *The Territorial Imperative.* New York: Atheneum, 1966.
———, *The Social Contract.* New York: Atheneum, 1970.

BAXTER, J.C., AND R.M. ROZELLE, "Nonverbal Expression as a Function of Crowding during a Simulated Police-Citizen Encounter," *Journal of Personality and Social Psychology,* 32, (1975), 40-54.

BYRNE, D., *The Attraction Paradigm.* New York: Academic, 1971.

EDNEY, J.J., "Human Territoriality," *Psychological Bulletin,* 81, (1974), 959-975.

EMILEY, S.F., "The Effects of Crowding and Interpersonal Attraction on Affective Responses, Task Performance, and Verbal Behavior," *Journal of Social Psychology,* 97, (1975), 267-278.

EOYANG, C.K., "Effects of Group Size and Privacy in Residential Crowding," *Journal of Personality and Social Psychology,* 30, (1974), 389-392.

FELIPE, N.J. AND R. SOMMER, "Invasions of Personal Space," *Social Problems,* 14, (1966), 206-214.

FISHER, J.D., "Situation-Specific Variables as Determinants of Perceived Environmental Aesthetic Quality and Perceived Crowdedness," *Journal of Research in Personality,* 8, (1974), 177-188.

HALL, E.T., *The Silent Language.* New York: Doubleday, 1959.

———, *The Hidden Dimension.* New York: Doubleday, 1966.

KNOWLES, E.S., et al., "Group Size and the Extension of Social Space Boundaries," *Journal of Personality and Social Psychology,* 33 (1976), 647-654.

LORENZ, K., *On Aggression.* New York: Harcourt, Brace, and Jovanovich, 1966.

MIDDLEMIST, R.D., E.S., KNOWLES, AND C.F. MATTER, "Personal Space Invasions in the Lavatory: Suggestive Evidence for Arousal," *Journal of Personality and Social Psychology,* 33 (1976), 541-546.

ROSENBLATT, P.C., AND L.G. BUDD, "Territoriality and Privacy in Married and Unmarried Cohabiting Couples," *Journal of Social Psychology,* 97 (1975), 67-76.

SMITH, S., and W.W. HAYTHORN, "Effects of Compatibility, Crowding, Group Size, and Leadership Seniority on Stress, Anxiety, Hostility, and Annoyance in Isolated Groups," *Journal of Personality and Social Psychology,* 22 (1972), 67-79.

SOMMER, R., "Studies in Personal Space," *Sociometry,* 22 (1959), 247-260.

———, *Personal Space.* Englewood Cliffs, Prentice-Hall, 1969.

STOKOLS, D., "On the Distinction between Density and Crowding: Some Implications for Future Research," *Psychological Review,* 79 (1972), 275-278.

SUNDSTROM, E., "An Experimental Study of Crowding: Effects of Room Size, Intrusion, and Goal Blocking on Nonverbal Behavior, Self-Disclosure, and Self-Reported Stress." *Journal of Personality and Social Psychology,* 32 (1975), 645-654.

THIBAUT, J.W., AND H.H. KELLEY, *The Social Psychology of Groups.* New York: Wiley, 1959.

TINBERGEN, N., "On War and Peace in Animals and Man." *Science,* 160 (1968), 1411-1416.

ZAJONC, R.B., "Attitudinal Effects of Mere Exposure." *Journal of Personality and Social Psychology,* 9(2), Part 2 (monograph), 1968.

ZLUTNIK, S., AND I. ALTMAN, "Crowding and Human Behavior," in J.F. Wohlwill and D.H. Carson, eds., *Environment and the Social Sciences: Perspectives and Applications.* Washington, D.C.: American Psychological Association, 1972.

Chapter 3

AIELLO, J.R., AND S.E. JONES, "Field Study of the Proxemic Behavior of Young School Children in Three Subcultural Groups," *Journal of Personality and Social Psychology,* 19 (1971), 351-356.

BAXTER, J.C., "Interpersonal Spacing in Natural Settings," *Sociometry,* 33 (1970), 444-456.

DOOLEY, B.B., "Crowding Stress: The Effects of Social Density on Men with 'Close' or 'Far' Personal Space" (unpublished Ph.D. dissertation, University of California at Los Angeles, 1974).

EPSTEIN, Y.M., AND R.A. KARLIN, "Effects of Acute Experimental Crowding," *Journal of Applied Social Psychology,* 5, (1975), 34-53.

GRUCHOW, H.W., "A Study of the Relationships between Catecholamine Production, Crowding, and Morbidity in Humans" (unpublished Ph.D. dissertation, University of Wisconsin, 1974).

HENDERSON, L.F., AND D.J. LYONS, "Sexual Differences in Human Crowd Motion," *Nature,* 240 (1972), 353-355.

LITTLE, K.B., "Cultural Variations in Social Schema," *Journal of Personality and Social Psychology,* 10 (1968), 1-7.

POLLIS, A., "Political Implications of the Modern Greek Concept of Self," *British Journal of Sociology,* 16 (1965), 29-47.

Ross, M., et al., "Affect, Facial Regard, and Reactions to Crowding," *Journal of Personality and Social Psychology,* 28 (1973), 69-76.

Szalai, A., editor, *The Use of Time.* The Hague: Mouton, 1972.

Schmidt, D.E., R.D., Goldman, and N.R. Feimer, "Physical and Psychological Factors Associated with Perceptions of Crowding: An Analysis of Subcultural Differences." *Journal of Applied Psychology,* 61, (1976), 279-289.

Stark, C.A., "The Effect of Crowding on One Aspect of Social Behaviour," *Journal of Behaviour Science,* 1 (1973), 367-368.

Vanderveer, R.B., "Privacy and the Use of Personal Space" (unpublished Ph.D. dissertation, Temple University, 1973).

Chapter 4

Belmont, L., and F.A. Marolla, "Birth Order, Family Size, and Intelligence," *Science,* 182, (1973), 1096-1101.

Bradley, R.H. and B.M. Caldwell, "The Relation of Infants' Home Environments to Mental Test Performance at Fifty-Four Months: A Follow-up Study," *Child Development,* 47 (1976), 1172-1174.

D'Atri, D.A., "Psychophysiological Responses to Crowding," *Environment and Behavior,* 7 (1975), 237-252.

Dennis, W., *Children of the Creche.* Englewood Cliffs, N.J.: Prentice-Hall, 1973.

Evans, G.W., "Behavioral and Physiological Consequences of Crowding in Humans" (unpublished Ph.D. dissertation, University of Massachusetts, 1975).

Freedman, J.L., *Crowding and Behavior.* San Francisco: Freeman, 1975.

Garber, H., and R. Heber, "The Milwaukee Project: Early Intervention as a Technique to Prevent Mental Retardation," in H.C. Lindgren, ed., *Children's Behavior.* Palo Alto: Mayfield, 1975.

Gray, S.W., and R.A. Klaus, "The Early Training Program: A Seventh Year Report," *Child Development,* 41 (1970), 909-924.

Greenberg, J.W., and H.H. Davidson, "Home Background and School Achievement of Black Urban Ghetto Children," *American Journal of Orthopsychiatry,* 42 (1972), 802-810.

HILLERY, J.M., AND S.S. FUGITA, "Group Size Effects in Employment Testing," *Educational and Psychological Measurement,* 35 (1975), 745-750.

HUNT, P.J., AND J.M. HILLERY, "Social Facilitation in a Coaction Setting: An Examination of the Effects over Learning Trials," *Journal of Experimental Social Psychology,* 9 (1973), 563-571.

MACCOBY, E.E., "Socialization Theory: Where Do We Go from Here?" (Presidential Address, Western Psychological Association, Sacramento, Ca., 1975).

McCAIN, G., V.C., COX, AND P.B. PAULUS, "The Relationship between Illness Complaints and Degree of Crowding in a Prison Environment," *Environment and Behavior,* 8 (1976), 283-290.

PAULUS, P.B., A.B., ANNIS, J.J., SETA, J.K. SCHKADE, AND R.W. MATTHEWS, "Density Does Affect Task Performance," *Journal of Personality and Social Psychology,* 34 (1976), 248-253.

RUTTER, M., B. YULE, O. QUINTON, W. YULE, AND M. BERGER, "Attainment and Adjustment in Two Geographical Areas: III. Some Factors Accounting for Area Differences," *British Journal of Psychiatry,* 126 (1975), 520-533.

SANDERS, G.S., and BARON, R.S. "The motivating effects of distraction on task performance." *Journal of Personality and Social Psychology,* 32 (1975), 956-963.

SHAPIRO, A.H., "Effects of Family Density and Mothers' Education on Preschoolers' Motor Skills," *Perceptual and Motor Skills,* 38 (1974), 79-86.

ZAJONC, R.B., "Family Configuration and Intelligence," *Science,* 192 (1976), 227-236.

Chapter 5

ADLER, R., *Speedboat,* pp. 3-4. New York: Random House, 1976.

ALEXANDER, C., "The City as a Mechanism for Sustaining Human Contact," in W. R. Ewald, Jr., ed., *Environment for Man: The Next Fifty Years,* 84, 93. Bloomington: Indiana University Press, 1967.

APPLEYARD, D., AND M. LINTELL, "The Environmental Quality of City

Streets: The Residents' Viewpoint," in W.J. Mitchell, ed., *Environmental Design: Research and Practice,* Proceedings of the Third Environmental Design Research Association Conference, University of California, Los Angeles, January, 1972.

BERLAND, T., *The Fight for Quiet,* p. 46. Englewood Cliffs, N.J.: Prentice-Hall, Inc., 1970.

BRAGDON, C.R., *Noise Pollution: The Unquiet Crisis.* Philadelphia: University of Pennsylvania Press, 1970.

BRIGGS, A., "The Sense of Place," in *The Fitness of Man's Environment,* pp. 79-97, Smithsonian Annual II. Washington, D.C.: Smithsonian Institution Press, 1968.

DARLEY, J.M., AND B. LATANÉ, "Bystander Intervention in Emergencies: Diffusion of Responsibility," *Journal of Personality and Social Psychology,* 8, no. 4 (1968), pp. 377-83.

DAVIS, K.A., *World Urbanization 1950-1970,* Vol. II. Berkeley: Institute of International Studies, 1972.

————, "The Urbanization of the Human Population," in *Cities,* pp. 3-24. New York: Alfred A. Knopf, 1966.

DUBOS, R., *Man Adapting,* p. 279. New Haven: Yale University Press, 1965.

FISCHER, C.S., *The Urban Experience.* New York: Harcourt, Brace, Jovanovich, 1976.

FRIED, M., "Grieving for a Lost Home," in L. Duhl, ed., *The Urban Condition,* pp. 151-71. New York: Basic Books, 1963.

GLOBE, E., "Lip Service to Noise Control," *Architectural Record,* 134 (November 1964), p. 11.

HUMPHREY, H.H., "Foreword," in *The Fitness of Man's Environment,* Smithsonian Annual II, Washington, D.C.: Smithsonian Institution Press, 1968.

ITTELSON, W.H., et al., *An Introduction to Environmental Psychology,* pp. 267-84. New York: Holt, Rinehart, and Winston, 1974.

JAMES, WM., *Psychology,* p. 179. Cleveland: World Publishing Co., 1948. (Reprint of 1890 edition.)

KAVALER, L., *Noise: The New Menace,* pp. 93-109. New York: John Day Co., 1974.

LATANÉ, B., AND J.M. DARLEY, *The Unresponsive Bystander.* New York: Appleton-Century-Crofts, 1970.

_____, "Bystander 'Apathy,' " *American Scientist,* 57, no. 2 (1969), p. 247.

LIPSCOMB, D.M., *Noise: The Unwanted Sounds,* p. 295. Chicago: Nelson-Hall Co., 1974.

LOFLAND, L., *A World of Strangers,* p. 178. New York: Basic Books, 1973.

LOUIS, A.M., "The Worst American City," *Harper's* (January 1975), p. 67.

LYNCH, K., *The Image of the City.* Cambridge, Mass.: M.I.T. and Harvard University Press, 1960.

MAYER, A., *The Urgent Future.* New York: McGraw-Hill Book Co., 1967.

McLEAN, E., AND TARNOPOLSKY, A., "Noise, Discomfort, and Mental Health," *Psychological Medicine,* 7 (1977), 19-62.

MEIER, R.F., *A Communications Theory of Urban Growth.* Cambridge: Mass.: M.I.T. Press, 1962.

MILGRAM, S., "The Experience of Living in Cities," *Science,* 176 (March 13, 1970).

MILLER, J.G., "Sensory Overloading," in B.E. Flaherty, ed., *Psychophysiological Aspects of Space Flight.* New York: Columbia University Press, 1961.

PARK, R.E., "The City: Suggestions for Investigation of Human Behavior in the Urban Environment," in R. Sennet, ed., *Classic Essays on the Culture of Cities,* pp. 91-130. New York; Appleton-Century-Crofts, 1969.

PICKARD, J.P., "U.S. Metropolitan Growth and Expansion 1970-2000," in S.M. Mazie, ed., *Population, Distribution and Policy,* Vol. V, Research Reports, U.S. Commission on Population Growth and the American Future. Washington; Government Printing Office, 1972.

PILIAVIN, J., J. RODIN, AND J.A. PILIAVIN, "Good Samaritanism: An Underground Phenomenon?" *Journal of Personality and Social Psychology,* 13 (December 1969), pp. 289-330.

RIESMAN, D., *The Lonely Crowd.* New Haven: Yale University Press, 1952.

SAARINEN, T., *Environmental Planning, Perception, and Behavior,* p. 134. Boston: Houghton Mifflin, 1976.

SIMMEL, G., *The Sociology of Georg Simmel,* K.H. Wolff, ed., New York: Macmillan Co., 1950.

SJOBERG, G., "The Origin and Evolution of Cities," in *Cities*, pp. 3-24 and 25-39, New York. Alfred A. Knopf, 1966.

SOMMER, R., *Personal Space: The Behavioral Basis of Design*, pp. 145, 154. Englewood Cliffs, N.J.: Prentice-Hall, 1969.

SPIVAK, J., "The Future Revised: Population of the World Growing Faster Than Experts Anticipated," *Wall Street Journal* (April 12, 1976).

STILL, H., *In Quest of Quiet*, p. 15. Harrisburg, Pa.: Stackpole Books, 1970.

STRAUSS, A., ed., *The American City: A Sourcebook of Urban Imagery.* Chicago: Aldine Publishing Co., 1968.

STRAUSS, A., *Images of the American City.* New York: Free Press of Glencoe, 1961.

TERKEL, S., *Division Street: America.* New York: Pantheon Books, 1967.

TORCHIA, J., "Mean Streets," *San Francisco Examiner* (December 21, 1976), p. 15.

U.S. News and World Report, "Are All Big Cities Doomed?" (April 5, 1976), p. 50.

WARD, B., *The Home of Man.* New York: W.W. Norton and Co., 1976.

ZELDIS, C., "Death on a Sunday Afternoon," *San Francisco Examiner* (December 30, 1976), p. 25.

ZIMBARDO, P.G., "The Human Choice: Individuation, Reason and Order vs. Deindividuation, Impulse and Chaos," in J. Helmer and N.A. Eddington, eds., *Urbanman: The Psychology of Urban Survival*, pp. 222-23. New York: The Free Press, 1973.

Chapter 6

BETTELHEIM, B., *Love Is Not Enough.* New York: Collier Books, 1965.

HALL, E.T., *The Hidden Dimension*, pp. 136, 137, New York: Anchor Books, 1969.

HELMER, J., AND N. EDDINGTON, eds., *Urbanman*, pp. 49-60. New York: The Free Press, 1973.

LIBERMAN, E.G., "The Queue: Anamnesis, diagnosis, therapy," *Soviet Review*, 9 (Winter 1968), pp. 12-16.

SCHWARTZ, B., *Queuing & Waiting: Studies in the Social Organization of Access and Delay.* University of Chicago Press, 1975.

SMITH, H., *The Russians,* pp. 84-86. New York: Ballantine Books, 1976.

Chapter 7

ALEXANDER, B.K., AND E.M., ROTH, "The Effects of Acute Crowding on Aggressive Behavior of Japanese Monkeys," *Behavior,* 39 (1971), 73-90.

ARDREY, R., *The Territorial Imperative.* New York: Dell Publishing Co., 1966.

CALHOUN, J.B., "Population Density and Social Pathology," *Scientific American,* 206 (1962), 139-148.

FREEDMAN, J.L. (1975) *Crowding and Behavior.* San Francisco: Freeman, 1975.

FREEDMAN, J.L. "The Effects of Population Density on Humans," in J. Fawcett, *Psychological Perspectives on Populations.* New York: Basic Books, 1972.

GALLE, O.R., W.R. GOVE, AND J.M. McPHERSON, "Population Density and Pathology: What Are the Relations for Man?" *Science, 176* (April, 1972), 23-30.

GRIFFITT, W., AND R. VEITCH, "Hot and Crowded," *Journal of Personality and Social Psychology,* 17(1) (1971), 92-98.

HALL, E.T., *The Hidden Dimension.* New York: Doubleday & Co., 1966.

HILDRETH, A.M., L.R. DEROGATIS, AND K. McCUSKER, "Body Buffer Zone and Violence: A Reassessment and Confirmation," *American Journal of Psychiatry,* 127 (June 1971), 127-128.

HUTT, C., AND W.C. McGREW, "Effects of Group Density upon Social Behavior in Humans," in *Changes in Behavior with Population Density,* symposium presented at the meeting of The Association for the Study of Behavior, Oxford, July 17-20, 1967.

HUTT, C., AND M. VAIZEY, "Differential Effects of Group Density on Social Behavior," *Nature,* (March 26, 1966), 1371-1372.

KINZEL, A.F., "Body-buffer Zone in Violent Prisoners," *American Journal of Psychiatry,* 127 (July 1970), 1.

LEVY, L., AND A. HERZOG, "Effects of Population density and Crowding on Health and Social Adaptation in the Netherlands," *Journal of Health and Social Behavior,* 15 (1974), 228-240.

LORENZ, K., *On Aggression.* New York: Harcourt Brace & World Inc., 1966.

Loo, C.M., "The Effects of Spatial Density on the Social Behavior of Children," *Journal of Applied Social Psychology,* 2(4) (1972), 372-381.

NEWMAN, O., "A Theory of Defensible Space," *Intellectual Digest,* 111(7) (1973), 57-64.

SCHMITT, R.C., "Density, Delinquency and Crime in Honolulu," *Sociology & Social Research,* 41 (1957), 274-276.

SOUTHWICK, C.H., "An Experimental Study of Intragroup Antagonistic Behavior in Rhesus Monkeys," *Behavior,* (1967), 182-209.

ZLUTNICK, S., AND I. ALTMAN, "Crowding and Human Behavior," *Crowding and Human Behavior in Environment and the Social Sciences.* J. Wohlwill, and D. Carson, eds. Washington, D.C.: American Psychological Association, 1972.

Chapter 8

ALTMAN, I., *The Environment and Social Behavior.* Monterey, Calif.: Brooks/Cole Publ. Co., 1975.

BRETT, G.Z., AND B. BENJAMIN, "Housing and Tuberculosis in a Mass Radiographic Survey," *British Journal of Preventive and Social Medicine,* 11, no. 1 (January 1957), p. 7.

CASSEL, J., "Health Consequences of Population Density and Crowding," in R. Gutman, ed., *People and Buildings.* New York: Basic Books, 1972.

CASSEL, J., AND H. TYROLER, "Epidemiological Studies of Culture Change," *Archives of Environmental Health,* 3 (1961), 25.

D'ATRI D.A., AND A.M. OSTFELD, "Stress, Crowding and Blood Pressure in Man," in Proceedings of the A.P.H.A. 116 (November 4-8, 1973).

D'ATRI, D.A., "Psychophysiological Responses to Crowding," *Environ-*

ment and Behavior, 7, no. 2 (June 1975), Sage Publications, Inc., pp. 237-252.

DUBOS, RENÉ, "The Human Environment in Technological Societies," *The Rockefeller Review,* July-August, 1968.

HENRY, J.P., J.P. MEEHAN, AND P.M. STEPHENS, "The Use of Psychosocial Stimuli to Induce Prolonged Systolic Hypertension in Mice," *Psychosomatic Medicine,* 29 (1967), 408-432.

HENRY, J.P., P.M. STEPHENS, J. AXELROD, AND R.A. MUELLER, "Effect of Psychosocial Stimulation on the Enzymes Involved in the Biosynthesis and Metabolism of Noradrenaline and Adrenaline." *Psychosomatic Medicine,* 33 (1971), 227-237.

HOLMES, THOMAS H., "Multidiscipline Studies of Tuberculosis," in Phineas J. Sparer, ed., *Personality Stress and Tuberculosis.* New York: Oxford University Press, 1956.

LUNDBERG, U., "Urban Commuting: Crowdedness and Catecholamine Excretion," *Journal of Human Stress* 2 (September 1976), 26-32.

MASON, J.W., "Psychoendocrine Approaches in Stress Research," *Medical Aspects of Stress in the Military Climate.* Washington, D.C.: U.S. Government Printing Office, 1965.

McCAIN, G., VERNE C. COX, AND PAUL B. PAULUS, "The Relationship between Illness Complaints and Degree of Crowding in a Prison Environment," *Environment and Behavior,* 8, no. 2, (June 1976), Sage Publications, Inc., pp. 283-289.

STEWART, G.T., AND A.W. VOORS, "Determinants of Sickness in Marine Recruits," *American Journal of Epidemiology,* 89, no. 3 (May 14, 1968), 254-263.

WELCH, B. L., "Psychophysiological Response to the Mean Level of Environmental Stimulation. A Theory of Environmental Integration," in *Symposium on Medical Aspects of Stress in the Military Climate,* Walter Reed Army Institute of Research, April, 1964.

Chapter 9

ARDREY, R. *The Territorial Imperative.* New York: Laurel Books, 1971.

COTTLE, J. , "Our Soul-Baring Orgy Destroys the Private Self," *Psychology Today* (October 1957a), 22-23, 87.

_____, "Exposing Ourselves in Public," *New Republic* (March 8, 1975b), 18-21.

EISELEY, L., *The Night Country*. New York: Charles Scribner's Sons, 1971.

GIBRAN, K. *The Prophet*. New York: Alfred A. Knopf, 1966.

GOFFMAN, E., *The Presentation of Self in Everyday Life*. Woodstock, N.Y.: Overlook Press, 1973.

HALL, E.T., *The Silent Language*. Greenwich, Conn.: Fawcett Publications, 1959.

_____, *The Hidden Dimension*. Garden City, N.Y.: Doubleday & Co., 1966.

KIRA, A., "Your Need for Privacy," *House & Garden*, (May 1973), 34, 215.

LOFLAND, L.H., *A World of Strangers: Order and Action in Urban Public Space*. New York: Basic Books, 1973.

MCGINLEY, P., *The Province of the Heart*. New York: Viking Press, 1959.

MURPHY, R.F., "Social Distance and the Veil," *American Anthropologist* 66 (1964), 1257-1264.

RAINES, J.C., *Attack on Privacy*. Valley Forge, Pa.: Judson Press, 1974.

SCHWARTZ, B., "The Social Psychology of Privacy," *American Journal of Sociology* 73 (May 1968), 741-754.

SIMMEL, A., "Privacy Is Not an Isolated Freedom," in J.R. Pennock and J.W. Chapman, eds., *Privacy*, pp. 71-88. New York: Atherton Press, 1971.

SIMMEL, G. *The Sociology of Georg Simmel*, Kurt Wolff, ed. Glencoe, Ill.: Free Press, 1950.

SISK, J.P., "In Praise of Privacy," *Harper's* (February, 1975), 100-107.

VIERECK, P., "The Unadjusted Man: Last Refuge of Civilization's Secret Fires," *Saturday Review*, (November 1, 1958), 13-15.

WESTIN, A.F., *Privacy and Freedom*. New York: Atheneum, 1967.

Index